PRAISE FOR THE I

"This is a GREAT book. Young people must learn a lot about finance because they will face tens of thousands of financial alternatives and much tougher economic conditions than previous generations. Our population is aging, which will be a larger burden on them as will the ever-growing government debt. The Kid$Vest Project provides the essentials that will help them better cope and hopefully prosper."

– Henry (Bud) Hebeler, President, Boeing Aerospace Division (retired); former MIT Sloan School Board Member; WSJ Retirement and Wealth Expert

"Thanks for sharing The Kid$Vest Project book with me - I think you are onto something here! If we truly want a better life for our children, our grandchildren, and our communities, we need to work together to help them become financially stable."

– Joyce Serido, Ph.D. Associate Professor, Family Social Science, University of Minnesota

"Today's youth do not have a strong understanding of budgeting, saving, and investing due to their lack of financial education. The Kid$Vest Project will help kids of all ages acquire the necessary skills to become financially secure throughout their lives."

–Dan Stoltz, President & CEO, Spire Credit Union"

"The Kid$Vest Project offers a platform that parents and teachers can use to help our children become financially secure. The book depicts an accurate account of child financial literacy in the U.S. and then advances helpful suggestions to get them started in the right financial direction.

During my fifty years in education, most of it teaching math, my curriculum seldom included anything about financial literacy for my students. Had I read this book earlier in my career, I would have applied many of these ideas to my teaching. Now, I will apply it to my grandchildren!"

– Nansee Greeley, Executive Director,
Minnesota Association of Independent Schools

"As an organization and individual who has committed more than 40 years to helping students become financially capable, I applaud the work of Greg Fouks and the Kid$Vest Project. There is great urgency to ensure that the next generation knows how to manage their money wisely and Kid$Vest shows great promise in motivating young people to make sound financial decisions."

– Bob Kaitz, President & CEO, BestPrep,
Minnesota Financial Literacy Organization

How parents, teachers, and communities inspire kids to budget, save, and invest in their dreams!

By Greg A. Fouks, HeadKid

ISBN: 978-0-9987094-0-6
ISBN: 978-0-9987094-1-3
Library of Congress Catalog Number: 2017906415

Printed in the United States of America
First Printing: 2017
21 20 19 18 17 5 4 3 2 1

Illustrated by Brent Larson

Published by:

To order: www.KidsVest.org

DEDICATED TO:

To Carver C. Fouks, my mentor, teacher, coach, and the best dad a kid could ever have. Although he left us sooner than we would have liked, his was a life well-lived. He exemplified respect, humility, integrity, and leadership qualities towards everyone each day. He touched the lives of thousands of students, athletes, friends, and family in ways that made us all better people. Thank you, DaD! And thanks also to my loving and supportive mom, who thankfully is still with us!

To Jan Rohs Fouks, my wife of more than forty years, thank you for keeping after me to complete *The Kid$Vest Project* and for loving me.

To Jamie and Britt, Marissa and Brett, my kids and their spouses, who allowed me to practice my ideas and compile research for *The Kid$Vest Project* and who, I'm proud to say, are putting its methods into practice.

To Emma, Payton, Cardin, and Ellis, my grand-daughters, who will benefit from the Kid$Vest strategies and their parent's guidance to grow up "financially secure."

And finally:

To all kids and their parents, who struggle every day to find their piece of the American Dream. May you all learn and practice your way to your own personal DreamLife!

MISSION

"Building youth wealth through financial education and investment action."

TABLE OF CONTENTS

Addendums:

AMERICA: THE GREATEST COUNTRY ON EARTH?

In the first episode of the successful series, *The News Room*, news anchor and star, Jeff Daniels, is asked by a fresh-faced college sophomore, "What makes America the greatest country on earth?" His accurate but caustic response gets the anchor some free time off, when he says, "No, America is not still the greatest country in the world, but it could be again."

He points out how our lackluster K-12 educational system compares internationally, especially in math and science, how deficient our healthcare system is in scope and reach, and a myriad of other statements that demonstrate America has lost its global standing as "the greatest country in the world."

This makes for great TV, but the accuracy of his statement should make all Americans uneasy. The fact is, many of our kids are losing their chance to attain the American Dream. They may not have the skills, education, or training necessary to compete for future jobs. Twenty percent don't graduate from high school, let alone college. There is an additional skill set where American kids lag their international peers. What is it? Financial literacy—how to budget, save, and invest their way to financial security. Too many of our kids, even those with degrees, are woefully in debt due to school loans and credit card expenses. Debts they may never be able to pay back. A recent cover article in Bloomberg Magazine shows a 23-year-old with

$90,000 school debt laughing about his inability to repay these loans. Not so funny to those who are working hard to pay their own debt, or to the rest of us who will ultimately pay!

And Bill Griffith, CNBC anchor, recently sarcastically suggested on air that we shouldn't worry about our kids' lack of financial education or knowledge about debt, because "they will eventually figure it out." Sorry, Bill, many American kids won't figure it out until it is too late. And by the time they do, most of them will have missed their opportunity for "financial happiness."

The brutal truth is that the majority of our kids don't have a clue about financial security or how to obtain it. Even sadder, neither do their parents! They are missing out daily on the benefits compound interest can have on their savings, investments, and careers. Perhaps Bill Griffith's children will be debt-free from college and credit card expenses because Bill has the means to assist them and the financial smarts to teach them, but millions of kids won't have these advantages.

Yes, the price of not learning **budgeting, saving, and investing techniques** at home and in our school system costs our youth their hope, and their chance at financial freedom. It is not their fault! A kid with a modest income and a pile of debt has little or no chance of building a wealth nest-egg for emergencies, homeownership, or retirement savings. Throw in a car loan, a mortgage, marriage, and possibly children, and our young adults may not be able to contribute to their IRAs or 401(k) plans until they are well into their twenties or thirties. This is a huge setback toward financial security and a massive drain on our economy! Is it any wonder why 56% of Americans in the workforce have less than $10,000 saved for retirement? The "wealth gap" this scenario has created is one factor why the growth of the middle class has been crushed.

All too soon America's debt-ridden kids will become retirees who continue to put financial stress on our social, welfare, and healthcare systems. It's truly a shame that our society and educational systems are not making it a priority to assist, educate, and show our kids the action steps they can use to create a better lifestyle. If we don't teach them how to succeed financially, many of them will not be able to make it on their own. And the entrepreneurial-minded kids, who are our future, may not turn to innovative or inspirational careers because they need to settle for lower paying jobs just to survive. This will certainly impact small business job growth, the true engine of the American economy.

The Kid$Vest Project will tackle these problems head on—in simple, short chapters that provide financial education and investment action steps that parents, teachers, and communities need to pass on to our kids. Section I, Chapters 1 & 2, focuses on *Financial Literacy Philosophy and Research*. Section II, Chapters 3-7, focuses on *Financial Health—Education and Action Steps*. In Chapter 3, The Kid$Vest Model presents a strategic plan that can be initiated for both individual kids and communities across America. Section III, Chapters 8 & 9, concludes with *What We*

All Can Do and Addendum 1, *The Kid$Vest Financial Binder*.

Together we might just be able to dust off our tarnished image and again see America as “that shining place on the hill,” our very own Camelot, regaining its standing as “the greatest country on earth!”

Greg A. Fouks
HeadKid at KidsVest.org
@GregAFouks
GAFouks@KidsVest.org

FINANCIAL LITERACY PHILOSOPHY AND RESEARCH

Chapter ONE

BLUEPRINT TO FINANCIAL SECURITY

Most parents dream that their children's lives will be better than their own, both academically and financially. Although they know personal wealth doesn't necessarily assure happiness, financial security does offer an easier path toward achieving the American Dream. Too many people have already lost this opportunity, and their children may as well, unless we make some drastic changes in our home and educational approach to financial learning. Politically, there is a great deal of unrest in the United States between the haves and have-nots, known as the “Wealth Gap.” You heard it from President Obama on CNBC, and more recently from presidential candidates Hillary Clinton and Donald Trump (now President) during their recent campaigns.

One school of economic thought, called the trickle-down theory, suggests that economic benefit provided to upper-income earners will help society in total. That is, wealth will trickle down to all levels of society from the top. Another theory suggests government expansion and higher taxes on business and the wealthy would be the better approach. We continuously manipulate our economy in good and bad times, depending on which political party or economic cycle is currently in vogue. Regardless of your economic bias or individual politics, it is true that Americans have over-consumed their way to huge deficits. Many of us have used credit cards to live lifestyles that are not affordable or sustainable, regardless of our income level. David Cay Johnston, in a recent article in Investopedia entitled, “Who’s getting richer? Hardly anyone,” notes that "American average income on tax returns has fallen since 2000 by $2,620, or almost 4%, to $65,021 in 2015, with only the highly educated and already well-off prospering."

The American Dream used to include a satisfying career, a family home, a quality education for our children, the ability to pay our debts, and live a comfortable retirement. This dream never meant we all would be corporate CEOs, live in mansions, send our kids to the most expensive schools, or indulge our every whim—like the *rich and famous*. The top 1% may be able to do all these things, but the rest of us cannot.

However, with the proper education, hard work, and a little luck, most of us can obtain financial independence. That still can mean a paid-off home (or working toward it), little or no debt, a great credit rating, and a financial portfolio that allows us to follow our dreams and passions throughout our lives. This is true only if we learn and apply budgeting, saving, and investing techniques to our daily lifestyle, and we start when we are young. Why? Because when we form habits as children, they typically become a fundamental part of our adult lives.

Yes, there are steps all of us can take to become more financially independent! Mind you, none come with quick fixes—there are no silver bullets to eliminate our 30-40 years of over-consumption and stagnant incomes. Going forward we must make the economic pie larger so more Americans can *play in the game*. *The Kid$Vest Project* is a simple (not easy), but life-changing method to increase the size of our economic pie. Its major goals include:

1. Establishing national financial literacy curriculum in grades K-12
2. Teaching kids budgeting, saving, and investment principles at home and in our schools
3. Enabling American teens to initiate investment action steps before age 20
4. Making sure all kids and parents, with and without means, are included in the strategy

Up until now, financial literacy training has often been attempted, but has typically neglected at least one or more of these four goals.

In other words, you can teach kids how to hit a baseball, but if you want them to be successful baseball players they must also consistently and correctly practice the skill on their own and against competition. And by successful, I don't mean becoming a Harmon Killebrew, Rod Carew, or Joe Mauer (Go Twins!). Only a few elite and talented individuals get to this skill level (top 1%) in any profession. Yet, we can all learn to swing a baseball bat better and get more enjoyment out of the game if we receive some coaching and then practice.

The same is true when teaching budgeting, saving, and investing (BSI) techniques—the guts of *The Kid$Vest Project*. We must first learn financial principles and then practice them to hone the necessary skills. In the book, *Outliers*, Malcolm Gladwell discusses factors that contribute to extraordinary levels of individual success. The "10,000-Hour Rule" suggests that the key to achieving world class expertise in any skill is, largely, a matter of correctly practicing for approximately 10,000 hours. Bill Gates and the Beatles are two examples of what happens when superior talent and practice collide. Mr. Gates played with computers and the Beatles played with music for extensive periods of time crafting their skills. Coaching without practice (action) offers our youth little chance at perfecting their baseball swing or becoming financially literate.

FINANCIAL LITERACY FAILURE

Dr. Lewis Mandell, former Dean of the School of Management at SUNY–Buffalo, and a Senior Fellow at the Aspen Institute, has studied financial literacy for years. He has concluded that financial literacy education, as currently taught, "does not work." Thus, challenging our educational systems to make financial literacy important in school curriculums must become a priority.

Teaching kids how to budget, save, and invest throughout their lives is not a onetime, or after-school-club event. While financial curriculum is not a new idea, we continue to execute it poorly in America. We need solid classroom financial education for grades K-12, just like we have in "reading, writing, and arithmetic." We should also take advantage of existing on-line and new web-based education techniques to teach financial literacy to broader groups of students. We need educational building blocks and repetition to hammer home these techniques until they become second nature to students—just like addition and subtraction.

Recently, I was surprised to find how well my nine-year-old granddaughter, Payton, already knows her multiplication tables. She was taught them in school, practiced them at home, and finally they earned a place in her memory bank. Now she needs to learn (which is a cinch, since I am her grandfather) that stock portfolios and watching bank statements grow are just as important and fun. Go Payton! It is important that every child learn what a positive impact financial education can have on their lives, yet, we rarely discuss it in our schools or at home. Even sex education is taught more frequently than financial education!

In fact, Heather Long's CNNMoney's article entitled, *Sex Ed is required. Why isn't financial education?* states that while "Sex education is mainstream in K-12 schools, financial education is not. The result is that the US ranks 14th behind Israel, Canada, Australia, Singapore, and much of Europe in financial literacy. The reason why this is a huge problem is because America places almost the entire burden of life's biggest financial decisions on the shoulders of individuals," i.e. our youth. Kids raised in middle or low income families especially need access to this kind of education to effectively equip them to compete financially in our society.

If you can believe it, only seventeen states in the United States require a financial literacy class before students graduate high school. And that is only a single class! While the states of Virginia, Utah, and a grassroots student group in Rhode Island are working to improve financial literacy in their schools, nationally we have a long way to go. Is it any wonder we have the financial problems we have?

You can't learn, understand, or practice what you haven't been taught.

Therefore, first, we must support and pressure our state legislatures, school boards, teachers, and their communities to realize the need for K-12 financial literacy education. Initiating curriculum with BSI knowledge and skill is critical to the overall financial success of our youth. Organizations already providing curriculum include: The National Endowment of Financial Education (NEFE), who provides free curriculum to schools, the National Financial Educators Council (NFEC), and the Council for Financial Education (CFE), who provide paid-for curriculum.

Second, as curriculum changes are made, we need to *teach the teachers* responsible for these subjects how to best implement financial information into their classrooms. Thankfully, numerous "maverick" teachers are already providing financial literacy information to their students because they understand this need. Subject matter that is meaningful and fun is key—so kids enjoy learning about their financial futures. And teachers don't have to be business teachers to incorporate financial curriculum in their classroom.

From my educational and training experience, I have learned that many teachers have strict curriculums they must follow, which limit additional topics they can introduce. Others may not have a strong background in finance and feel challenged to present the information to students. This is simply human nature! The Council for Economic Education (CEE) is an organization that offers financial literacy to educators by "*teaching the teachers*," as well as providing curriculum to students. In my home state of Minnesota, BestPrep also provides programs that *train the trainers* in financial literacy. This kind of financial education and teacher training must become mainstream in our national education systems.

Third, and most important, we need to show financially educated kids how to fund their saving, investment, and retirement plans (Roth IRAs). It is the ultimate practice and application of their knowledge that promotes real understanding—and results. Without action and application, kids just don't retain the knowledge they've learned. *Use it or lose it*. That's why University of Minnesota financial literacy researcher Joyce Serido suggests, "knowledge is not behavior. You may know what you should do, but feeling confident in moving forward and making decisions that are best for you—that is capability."

It is also why the financial education author and trainer Sam Renick said, "Saving money is the most important lesson parents should teach kids under five years old." We'll discuss this topic in more detail in future chapters, but for now let me give you an example.

Let's assume that a teenager with a part-time, or full-time, job has learned BSI techniques. This enlightened kid socks away a modest $250 per year ($20 per month or one less latte per week) in a Roth IRA for four years before she graduates high school.

This $1,000 outlay could be the best investment she will ever make in her future!

Why? Because that $1,000 could be worth approximately $60,000-90,000 tax free in 40-45 years. That's right, even if she never contributes another dime, she still will have a base of financial security. And if she can add more dollars, the numbers can be even larger.

Of course, investing $1,000 dollars over four years may be a challenge for some teens. But remember, contributions can also be supplemented by you or grandma/grandpa. Yes, parents can make contributions in their kid's name for any hours they work. And birthday or graduation gifts could add to their Roth IRA. Bottom line, any amount contributed during their teens sets your kids on the road to financial security and creates a successful pattern of saving. What a great habit to initiate!

While kids won't become wealthy overnight, the knowledge and satisfaction of watching their investment portfolio grow throughout their lives can positively change the way they think about themselves and their careers. For those working students, parents, and grandparents who can't afford this approach due to financial constraints, I offer a potential strategy your community can initiate via *The Kid$Vest Model* in Chapter three.

An additional strategy would be for a kid to take a "gap year" after high school. A gap year is the popular term for taking a year off between high school and college. Kids can travel, learn about their passions and strengths, or simply have some fun. Malia Obama, daughter of President Obama, is traveling for a year before she attends Harvard in the fall of 2017. Not a bad idea, if you or your parents can fund this type of sabbatical.

However, if your kid isn't sure he is college material, he doesn't have an exact career plan, or the funds to pay for college (and you can't help), how about persuading him to try a gap year and work? The money earned during their "working gap year" could fund their Roth IRA (priority), add to college savings, or pay for a host of other expenses they might have compiled. There is nothing wrong with this approach. After all, your kids are likely going to work for more than forty years. This is an especially good idea if they have the luxury of living at home. Also, a reasonably good, or even higher paying job might be available as well, since they won't be competing against those peers who are starting college right away.

And here's the final reason *The Kid$Vest Project* is so important. If we teach financial literacy to our youth and help them take action steps early enough, they will likely continue to apply this knowledge as adults. They will have built up thousands more in saving, emergency funds, and retirement dollars (via IRAs or 401(k)s) by the time they reach sixty. And they don't have to wait 40 years before their lives change dramatically. You see, as these kids watch their savings and investments grow during their thirties, forties, and fifties, the choices they will have regarding work, vacations, hobbies, and retirement can be dramatically different. Imagine taking on a career or hobby they desire and that satisfies them as they age, versus a job they need for a paycheck. Or knowing that in retirement they can continue a way of life they enjoy because they have earned a future paycheck.

Think about it—all kids who participate in Kid$Vest strategies can have an equal opportunity to build wealth regardless of whether they go/don't go to college, or whether they become custodians, teachers, scientists, or CEOs. This also puts less stress on our government and social organizations like Welfare, Social Security, and Medicare. And perhaps one day down the road, these financially smart kids will become well-to-do adults who can pay-it-forward to future generations of Americans!

Thus, only a consistent day-in and day-out education and action program can truly solve the poor financial literacy skills of our American youth. Or as Annamaria Lusardi, a professor at George Washington University, and one of the leading experts on financial literacy, suggests that "Any year we delay by not adding financial education, one more generation is going out of high school without those skills and knowledge." Remember, without incorporating all four above mentioned goals into a financial literacy program, America will continue to support a band-aid approach that only shows modest results. The Kid$Vest Project can greatly improve financial outcomes for kids of all economic levels.

COMPOUNDING MIRACLE

So what is the financial fuel that allows our kids saving and investment engines to start? As Albert Einstein suggested, "it's the Miracle of Compound Interest." N.S. Williams of Baltimore, MD offers the following example of compounding at its finest.

> *"I can do you one better on the compound interest route to riches. If, the day you were born, someone put one dollar a day in a box for you, at age 65 you would have about $25,000 in the box. Had that same dollar a day been put into a pass book account that paid 3%, at the end of the same 65*

years you would have $75,000. At 5% interest, your dollar a day would have grown to almost $200,000. Now we are beginning to talk about some real money. If an investment of 10% was utilized, your dollar per day would grow into a staggering $2.75 million." And if you wanted to dream......

I could continue Mr. William's example, but you get the point! Kids (or their parents) who don't understand or take advantage of compound interest miss out on hundreds of thousands of dollars more in investment earnings over their lives, simply because they didn't start saving early or often enough.

The GoBankingRates table below shows a second compounding example. It shares how much money individuals would need to put aside each month, based on their ages, and the rate of return, to accumulate $1 million dollars at retirement. Clearly the table shows that the rate of return percent has a huge impact on the overall savings, but early saving is the real key for more retirement dollars. Since we can't control what the interest rate will be, the only variable we can control is how early we start saving.

Monthly dollars at various ages and interest rates to save $1,000,000.					
Age	2% Rate	7% Rate	8% Rate	9% Rate	10% Rate
20	$1,143.31	$263.67	$189.59	$135.05	$95.40
25	$1,361.59	$380.98	$286.45	$213.61	$158.13
30	$1,645.96	$555.23	$435.94	$339.93	$263.39
35	$2,029.53	$819.69	$670.98	$546.23	$442.38
40	$2,571.88	$1,234.46	$1,051.50	$891.96	$753.67
45	$3,392.17	$1,919.66	$1,697.73	$1,497.26	$1,316.88
50	$4,768.42	$3,154.95	$2,889.85	$2,642.67	$2,412.72

Table 1

For example, when you are 20 years old you must save $190 a month at 8% to reach the $1 million level, while at age 40 you must save over $1,000 per month to achieve the same $1 million dollars. Compound interest, baby! We will come back to the miracle of compound interest in Chapter Six, entitled *Just for Fun, How to Become a Millionaire.*

Kid$Vest is but one idea I think former Apple founder Steve Jobs might call “INSANELY GREAT” in helping all our kids succeed. I want to live in an enlightened America—where everyone truly has an equal opportunity to learn and apply BSI techniques to become financial secure. This could mean a fulfilling career, little or no debt, and the ability to give back to society through service or philanthropy.

Whatever else kids do in their lives, those who take advantage of *The Kid$Vest Project* techniques will have earned a solid financial base that puts them on their own personal road toward "financial freedom." That is life changing—the true American Dream. I'd like a piece of this kind of American economic pie. How about you?

"I believe strongly in the ability of kids—all kids!"

Michelle Rhee
Founder, *Students first.org*
Former Superintendent,
Washington DC Schools

Chapter

TWO

THE NEED FOR YOUTH FINANCIAL LITERACY

At a recent Sunday dinner, my youngest sister, her 20-year-old son and I were discussing financial literacy and investing. By now you know my enthusiasm for this subject. My passion led me to ask them questions about their financial knowledge. I asked my nephew if he had taken any personal finance courses in school. Then I asked my sister, a successful twenty-year veteran kindergarten teacher in a local school, about her school's curriculum regarding financial literacy. It came as no surprise to me even though he was a junior in college, Jeffrey had received no financial literacy training in school at any2017. level. Also, my sister had never been given any financial curriculum guidelines for her classroom.

She took it upon herself to use a hypothetical shopping game with her kindergarten class. I was amazed at how sophisticated her training module was about budgeting and resource allocation for kids this young. No doubt this is why she is an excellent teacher—she intuitively knows how important this subject is to even her youngest students. Of course, my nephew, a bright, conservative, and happy-go-lucky student had no idea of the positive impact he could have on his life and career if he started his Roth IRA immediately. He also didn't understand how compound interest really works. Nor did his mom! Unfortunately, this regrettable situation is typical of our educational training in the United States. However, I am happy to report that after our conversation, my nephew has now initiated a Roth IRA. Well done Jeffrey!

You may, or may not agree with my hypothesis that *The Kid$Vest Project* is an example of how we can change our youths' habits and lives by including financial education and action steps into their daily routines. You may not agree that long-term economic success and reduction of the wealth gap can be a positive outcome of its implementation over time. Well, I sincerely hope that reading *The Kid$Vest Project* changes your mind! Here are a few simple facts that clearly show the disastrous effect of what poor financial knowledge and insufficient retirement planning have already done to America's work force and our youth.

- The average American worker has $53,000 saved for retirement and over 50% of workers (75 million people) have saved nothing.
- The average college student graduates with $41,000 worth of school loans (debt) and $4,000 worth of credit card debt—you can double this if they go to grad school.
- A Schwab/Age Wave survey conducted with American kids grades the investing education they received from their parents at a C-, stating, “They didn’t know enough about investing to teach them anything.”
- The JumpStart Coalition found that less than 50% of high school seniors passed a basic financial literacy test, and just 62% of college seniors passed the same test. These rates translate into poor money management habits in adulthood.
- More than 70% of Americans know they cannot retire or lack the money to do so, and 35% of Americans over age 65 rely entirely on social security payments to live on.
- About 19% of workers have been compelled to take money from their retirement savings during the last year to cover urgent financial needs.
- The US middle class is stagnating; wage growth for the past thirty years is flat, and yet we continue to spend and use debt to maintain a standard of living we feel we deserve.
- Of the $1.3 trillion dollars in current student loan debt, 43% or roughly 22 million Americans

with federal student loans are not making payments, or are in default.

- The US fiscal budget deficit is huge (roughly $20 trillion) and cuts or changes will likely be made in Social Security, Medicare, and Medicaid, as well as other social services.

I don't know about you, but this devastating information blows me away! In my view, our lack of financial literacy training and investment action ranks right up there with terrorism and cybersecurity as threats to our American way of life. Our youths' financial neglect is detrimental to future generations because it is ripping the soul out of kids still trying to achieve the American Dream.

Yes, there is a tremendous need for any organization that can consistently and methodically teach kids financial truths and then offer them a vehicle by which they can begin their investment careers. Unfortunately, too many older Americans no longer have the time to change their futures. Let's not let this happen to our kids and future generations!

We have approximately 20 million American kids between the ages of sixteen and nineteen, and the clear majority don't know the value of saving, investing, or the miracle of compound interest. So says the Council for Economic Education in its *2016 Survey of the States*. Annamaria Lusardi, Ph.D., Denit Trust Chair of Economics at George Washington University School of Business, in the survey's commentary states, "This data is a call to action. We know now that most students are not financially literate; they lack this basic but fundamental skill to live in the 21st century. Ask for (financial programs) in your school districts and encourage your business community to support the training of teachers. Everyone will benefit from higher financial literacy for the young."

Our current generation of kids may not be like previous generations who entered a workforce with plentiful high paying jobs. Nor will they have defined benefit pensions that will pay them a percentage of their monthly income for life during retirement. No, this generation (whether Gen X or Millennials) are workforce mobile, technologically savvy, often geographically virtual, and rely on retirement vehicles like IRAs and 401(k)s for their retirement incomes. They receive little corporate support, unless they receive company matching in their 401(k) or profit sharing account. The bottom line—what they save in their individual retirement plan is what they can take out, plus Social Security (if it still exists). So far what our younger generation is saving or putting away to fund retirement programs is underwhelming. Yet there is still time for them!

Frankly, the US transition to 401(k)s and IRAs has been an abject failure for most worker retirement portfolios. Some reasons why employees don't get much bang for their retirement plan buck include:

- Roth IRAs and the 401(k) system are voluntary
- Plans often include high fees and fund costs
- Employees lack quality fund choices
- Small investors overpay in fees

- Employees often over-rely on company stock in their funds
- And finally, too many employers don't offer retirement programs

Throw in a healthy dose of employee procrastination for setting aside enough retirement dollars, or selecting funds that are way too conservative, and we begin to understand the dilemma. Also, a recent study by the Census Bureau notes that more than 66% of workers who have access to 401(k)s and other retirement vehicles are not using them. Worse, only 14% of private companies actually offer these types of retirement plans. This data was gathered by analyzing tax records vs. surveys, and is far lower than previous estimates show. Kid$Vest does not want this same scenario playing out with our current and future generations of kids.

As parents, we don't always know how motivated our kids will be, what grades they will obtain in school, where they will go to college or trade school, if they will graduate, or what career they may choose. In short, how successful will they become? But it seems to me that if we have our kids learn and practice a financial education plan at home and in school, and then initiate action steps (Roth IRA contributions) in their late teens and early twenties, they can obtain a solid level of financial security. *Now that is truly inspirational!*

PSYCHOLOGICAL & FINANCIAL LITERACY RESEARCH

For a moment, let's take a step back and include "successful learning" and financial literacy research that may lend positive support to *The Kid$Vest Project*. Numerous journalists and social psychologists have written about the psychology and science aspect behind successful learning. Most notably, David Brooks of the New York Times, discussed Walter Mischel's famous marshmallow experiment. Four-year old kids are left in a room with a bell and a marshmallow and they have two choices—ring the bell and Mischel will come back in and they can eat the one marshmallow, or wait till he returns on his own, and they will get two marshmallows.

The study is about instant gratification, or as economists say, 'present bias.' Remember buying that new pair of Nikes, the new flat screen TV, or that first car you couldn't live without? As we know, a certain percentage of kids have the willpower to resist ringing the bell, earning two marshmallows as their reward. However, some kids cannot wait. We see many children in this group pushing the marshmallow away but then in frustration ringing the bell - earning just one marshmallow. Most interesting, is that Mischel studied these kids over time. He found that the kids who had better self-control (who didn't ring the bell), also did better on college SAT scores, got into better colleges and had in general, better adult financial outcomes. That is, they have a better chance of becoming financially secure.

Mr. Brooks went on to say that “kids in poorer families are not especially good at delayed gratification. However, we can re-train ourselves to be better at delayed gratification by becoming aware of our self-control reactions and learning distraction techniques. Thus, instead of an educational system that uses structural reforms like class-size reduction or increased teacher pay, we should also be incorporating self-control techniques into our curriculums. Without doing so, we really aren't getting to the underlying problems.” Mr. Brooks makes a valid point, but any teachers whose class sizes have grown from 20 to 30 students and have growing family bills to pay, may have slightly different reactions to his comments.

Brooks concluded his article with comments from the book “The Happiness Hypothesis” by Jonathan Haidt. Haidt suggests that “what works is creating stable, predictable environments for children, in which good behavior pays off—and practice. Young people who are given a series of tests that demand self-control get better at it over time.”

I guess I was one of the lucky kids with parents who taught self-control, or maybe I was just hard-wired that way. Either way, the Fouks kids learned to be frugal because with Dad teaching and coaching, and Mom at home with five kids, we simply didn't have much in the way of financial means. In fact, I clearly remember my mom and dad parking their car next to Mears Park in downtown St. Paul when I was 8 or 9 years old. While we played in the park, Dad went into an office building to take out a $400 loan for a refrigerator.

However, what we did have were loving parents who were terrific role models. They respected others, worked extremely hard, and provided for all our needs—not necessarily all our wants. We learned the difference between wants and needs. I felt lucky, and so did my brother and sisters, because we thought we had a great life. And relative to many others in the community, we were very fortunate. Perhaps ignorance is bliss, but I think there was more to it than that.

When it comes to Haidt's comment about "good behavior and practice paying off," I know something about this too. Growing up the son of an excellent basketball and football coach, after school I spent hours at his practices shooting a ball or throwing a football with my brother and friends. It was a great break for my mom as she knew exactly where we were and what we were doing.

Yet, I always was amused when friends talked to me in high school about my natural ability to throw, shoot, and pass the ball. I'd laugh and agree that I certainly had some God-given talent. Nobody saw the thousands of hours I spent strategically watching my dad's practices and shooting over 500 basketball shots per night. Some skill and talent sure, but hard work and practice were just as big a part of my success. I was honing my skills and staying out of trouble. I knew even then I would never be in the NBA, but a scholarship did pay for college because of those long, enjoyable hours spent in the gym. It was a nice trade off in my mind! Somewhere Malcolm Gladwell, *Outliers* author, must be smiling.

Additionally, from the article *Rethinking How Students Succeed*, published in the 2015 Stanford Social Innovation Review, "we understand what it takes to become 'effective learners'—students who develop a set of qualities that include self-control, persistence, social awareness, relationship skills, curiosity, resilience, and self-confidence. However, in their quest to do better, educators typically focus on improving their skills at teaching core subjects, such as reading, math, and science. But research shows that students who develop social and emotional learning (SEL) skills and academic mindsets do better in school. The potential for schools to foster more effective learners has not been developed to any significant scale, especially for students from low-income districts who would benefit the most."

Finally, a recent study in 2016 by PwC (Price Waterhouse Coopers) and the George Washington University, entitled *Millennials and Financial, Literacy—The Struggle with Personal Finance,* suggests that Millennials' (ages 23-35) financial illiteracy could be disastrous for the economy. They note that "Only 24% demonstrated basic financial knowledge and only 8% demonstrated high financial literacy." The report went on to say that "Millennials owe a lot. They know too little. Their struggle with debt may eventually become our problem, too."

In conclusion, here is what we do know:

- The home is not a place where kids typically learn or practice financial literacy

- Our national and state education associations include very little, if any core financial literacy education or application of successful learning principles in current curriculums
- Most teachers don't include consistent financial literacy or current successful learning techniques in their classrooms, nor have they been adequately trained to do so
- Most organizations offering financial literacy training are typically one-time events or short modules that don't create successful financial habits

Basically, our kids are left to figure out how to budget, save, and invest for their financial futures almost entirely on their own. They are paying, and will continue to pay, a harsh penalty from this "school of hard knocks" experiential learning. Even worse, by the time they head off to college or work, they often must make big spending decisions involving thousands of dollars, which may affect their entire lives. Many of these decisions are ones they have not been educated or trained to make.

We have the research and empirical evidence to understand what is necessary to improve our kids' general and financial educations. Should anyone be surprised, however, that a generation of parents or teachers who lacked financial literacy training in their own youth are not passing great financial guidance on to their kids? Of course not! And how can we expect our kids to take advantage of the compound interest miracle when fewer than half of our states provide only one personal finance course in senior high? The education and action step failures we continue to make in America are a disservice to our youth, especially our disadvantaged youth.

While all career choices might not be of a similar caliber, with the proper education and action steps, people in all walks of life can achieve success. We can certainly upgrade our math, science, engineering, and technology (STEM) programs, and add social and emotional learning (SEL) modules around the softer skills. They are very important in the development of our kid's minds. But let's not forget the positive role financial literacy can have on our kids or in the growth of a vibrant middle class. American education needs to include this skill set in their priorities to break this horrific cycle!

"You can't always get what you want, but if you try, sometimes you might just get what you need."

Mick Jagger

FINANCIAL HEALTH-EDUCATION AND ACTION STEPS

Chapter THREE

THE KID$VEST MODEL

Kid$Vest's plan is to assist parents and teachers financially educate kids and then help them take action.

Our approach allows young people to become fiscally responsible early in life so they can become financially independent later in life.

You don't have to look very hard to find numerous articles and books pertaining to financial literacy, debt, and retirement. Reporters and financial gurus frequently share on-line ideas or tactics on how to attain financial wealth. I read an article every day on MSN, *The Star Tribune* (Minneapolis local paper),

Morningstar, The Wall Street Journal or *MoneyTalks News* (Stacy Johnson's excellent blog) discussing budgeting, saving, debt reduction, and the death of the American Dream. Most are very well written and the advice offered is sound.

There are also existing non-profit organizations providing kids and school systems with personal finance information and programs. JumpStart, Junior Achievement, and BestPrep in Minnesota are just a few of these programs. Any individual or group whose passion is to teach BSI techniques to our kids is a friend of Kid$Vest. We wholeheartedly support all these organizations, whether they are working philanthropically or for profit! They all offer advice and examples that afford our kids a better future.

Still these individuals, organizations, and our education systems lack the coordinated effort (especially during K-12) that would guide more of our youth to become financially secure.

And action steps are mostly non-existent.

That is exactly why the Consumer Financial Protection Bureau and the Center for Financial Services Innovation now prefer the term *Financial Health* to financial literacy. Accordingly, the two fundamentals *The Kid$Vest Project* advocates in correcting American kids' financial health inadequacies include:

1. Increased financial education at home and in school curriculums—so they know what and how to do.
2. Action steps to reinforce positive behavior and obtain long term results—so they actually do.

The Kid$Vest Vision

My financial health philosophy supports gradual but constant emersion of personal finance topics from grades K-7. Financial modules that are fun and keep young kids interested are important, but we need to continue to increase their scope and sophistication as they age. By the time our kids leave the seventh grade, they should understand budgeting, be able to make savings and investment decisions, and grasp the psychology of instant versus delayed gratification, compound interest and how financial success can lead them to financial security. This is most certainly not happening now!

Then from 8-12th grade, teachers can expand the financial modules and offer at least two stand-alone Personal Finance Classes featuring BSI practices. For instance, how taxes and debt (car, student, home, credit card) affect their net worth. Also, they should understand financial instruments like stocks, bonds, insurance, and real estate, which will affect their investment and retirement programs throughout their life. These classes must be an integral part of our school curriculum, like we already do with our Science, Technology, Engineering, and Math (STEM) subjects.

If you are going to make financial literacy "top of mind," you can't provide sporadic after school activities or offer a one-time senior high class before graduation. We already know this method of financial education does not provide successful outcomes for our kids. My friend, Dr. Lewis Mandell, Ph.D., University of Washington, concludes that "financial education, as currently administered, does not appear to have any lasting impact...current methods don't work."

What does it mean when I say that action steps are the missing link or key to achieving financial results? So far, I haven't clearly defined them, other than kids establishing a Roth IRA in their teens. Of course, a Roth IRA is still the ultimate action step of *The Kid$Vest Project*. But incremental events and conversations at home and in school can logically guide kids toward this most important goal. Think of these action steps as teachable moments in a child's life. Some action steps or financial building block examples include:

- Initiating a college 529 savings plan for a child at birth and talking to them about the plan as they grow-up.
- Having family dinner table discussions about money—BSI, needs vs. wants, etc. (Not every night!)
- Taking trips together to the grocery store or to the auto mechanic so kids can experience how their parents handle real-life situations.
- Playing games like Monopoly, Risk or Cribbage for family fun and financial education.

- Offering allowances based on work efforts at home and then showing kids how to allocate their income for BSI programs.
- Providing kids financial or business books and articles to be read and studied at home and in the classroom—including *The Kid$Vest Project*.
- Encouraging them to think about entrepreneurial ideas such as lemonade stands, paper routes, or lawn mowing services, especially when they show interest in such endeavors.
- Promoting BSI discussions as the kids earn income from part-time or full-time jobs.
- Helping them obtain a credit card that must be paid off monthly to educate kids about debt and credit establishment—but only if they are financially capable.
- Conducting discussions about important expenses such as cars and college, so kids participate in decisions that will affect their lives.
- Helping kids understand their individual strengths, gifts, and passions, so career and trade school discussions are more meaningful and productive.
- Discussing career and potential gap year decisions.
- Playing the 'match game' with your kids, if you can afford it. Whatever they save in a summer or annually, match their funds in their savings and/or Roth IRA accounts. This is a family at its best!

- Playing stock market, business, and entrepreneur games. Leading by example!
- Helping kids start a brokerage account and play with a few stocks of their choice—i.e. Disney, Nike, Google, or Facebook.
- Applying the principles of *The Kid$Vest Financial Binder* at least annually (Addendum 1).
- And ultimately, showing and teaching kids the value of hard work and the importance of working part or full-time in their teens—with some of the money going into their Roth IRA.

Parents and teachers can best decide how to discuss or implement these subjects at the dinner table or in the classroom. And please feel free to come up with additional action steps you think are important, as my list is certainly not all encompassing.

To be sure, the listed action steps above are not groundbreaking or profound. They are simply useful building blocks, so kids obtain a solid financial foundation. Like all learned skills, the more often financial education is discussed and repeated, the more knowledge and retention of the concepts are ingrained. And importantly, the more likely they will be applied. A great plan without implementation still ends up in failure.

Bottom line, financial knowledge by itself, without financial and investment implementation or action, only affords our youth to dream of financial security—not actually obtain it.

If there is no "pot of gold at the end of the rainbow," most kids will lose interest or not commit to an action plan. This could make all the difference in their financial success, especially when they want to retire in forty-fifty years. And why is this? Let's all say it together, please. It's because of the miracle of compound interest. Or, as the author of the book, *Warren Buffett Ground Rules,* Jeremy Miller, says, "Compound interest can make anyone a long-term winner."

Why should anyone believe my disruptive theories regarding financial health? I certainly don't have a purely academic background or a research Ph.D. behind my name. First, America's current financial literacy education is not working. That is obvious to anyone who is paying attention.

Second, I've been thinking about the lack of financial education, training, and action in my own life for years, and how things haven't changed much for my kids and their kids. I have been copying, saving, and sending financial literacy articles to my family and friends for more than 15 years. Parents and teachers continuously complain to me about their own kids' lack of BIS knowledge or training, when the subject comes up in conversation. This is tragic!

Third, and most significant, my unusual and circuitous work history in business, performance improvement, and as an entrepreneur has allowed me to make some personal discoveries about training and learning. For example, one of my first promotions was with Minnesota Mutual Life (Securian Financial). After a successful group sales stint, I was asked to come back to the home office to help senior sales management run 26 regional group offices. I was also responsible for managing the training program for new reps (along with my friend and co-worker, Dale McNaughton). I was very interested in cataloging what characteristics a good sales person needed to be successful, and what training techniques could offer quicker on-the-job success once someone was hired. Curiosity, and my upbringing drove me to find answers to develop the best training program possible.

To identify successful sales traits, I uncovered a study (this was 1979) from Herbert M. and Jeanne Greenberg (Personality Dynamics, a Princeton, New Jersey, consulting firm, in the Harvard Business Review). Their study suggested ego-centrism, ego drive and empathy were three highly correlated factors toward sales success. We carefully screened candidate resumes, their personal backgrounds, and then designed interview questions to score candidates on these three characteristics before making hiring decisions. We then aggressively trained these representatives about our products and sales techniques. We had recruits practice their sales presentations daily during the 4-month training program (their action step). These 'rookie reps' gave simulated presentations to each other and in group settings. Over time they became quite proficient with their polished sales pitches.

After training had concluded, we sent them to one of 26 regional group offices. These offices already had a manager and likely two to four representatives. As you might expect, the training they received in this real-world environment was often variable, due to the skill level of their sales manager and peers. But the real world also offered truths you can't teach in a controlled setting. Not surprisingly, we found that if you hired talented people on the front end by matching successful sales criteria, and then trained them well, they became successful sooner. This made their sales managers happy and the job more satisfying to the sales reps as well.

Imagine, these new reps produced more results and stayed longer. What a concept! As a matter of fact, we kept approximately seven of ten reps per year for an average of four to five years. This was a good return on field force numbers, especially when compared to previous classes where there was over 50% turnover in three years.

It sounds like *The Kid$Vest Project*, doesn't it? First, educate and then take investment action. As it turns out, recent studies about learning now agree with my simple hypothesis. My training background and the opportunity to 'give back' have led me to the development of the Kid$Vest concept over the past ten to fifteen years. Perhaps my experience has allowed me to gain some insight toward developing a model to financially assist our youth.

Kid$Vest.org

I'm hopeful this book, *The Kid$Vest Project,* eventually starts a groundswell of parents, teachers, and communities who provide financial health advice at home and in classrooms all over America. Yet, waiting for this to happen is not fair to our current or future generations of kids. Too many of them will have missed their opportunity for financial security. So, we have two approaches that can immediately begin changing kid's lives.

The first approach, and the coolest part of Kid$Vest is that no individual kid must wait for financial education to start popping up at home or in their classrooms. All they need to do is find their way to Kid$Vest.org—the one-stop website where member kids, parents, and teachers can go to access free financial education. We hope parents and teachers reading *The Kid$Vest Project* will guide, push, or shove their kids to this site. Or perhaps you and your kids can view and learn the financial information presented together. You know the old saying, "The family that plays together, stays together."

Kid$Vest.org can be the place where kids can strategically pursue their own individual DreamLife (chapter four). By obtaining financial knowledge and skills, I believe kids will learn how to live below their means and avoid some "present bias" mistakes. And of course, they can also establish their priority action step (Roth IRA) and begin taking advantage of the compound interest miracle.

Why is *now* the best time for kids to learn and apply financial knowledge? When kids are between the ages of five and eighteen years old, they usually have limited debt and expenses. And college loans are still on the distant horizon. Their expenses are often the lowest they will be during their entire lifetimes. This is true because parents typically shield them from the larger expenses such as healthcare etc., at least until they go out on their own. This is an ideal time for parents and teachers (or Kid$Vest.org) to guide their kids and students towards financial freedom. A window of opportunity exists that we don't want kids to miss. Like viewing autumn's colorful leaves, if you wait till the wind starts howling, the opportunity is lost—it's too late to capture the moment!

However kids discover the Kid$Vest organization, they can all become Kid$Club Members simply by signing up. For free! They can all learn, engage, and financially grow together. There is strength in numbers as kids of different geographies, and economic levels watch their peers succeed. Inspirational and heart-breaking stories from member kids and young adults should make all of us wiser and more confident about achieving our own financial security.

For the few kids who already are financially savvy, or have learned some monetary skills at home or in school, becoming a Kid$Club member and initiating their first Roth IRA is a no-brainer. I wish there were millions of kids already out there in this exact position, but I know better. Remember, the only legal restrictions are that they must work at least part time to make funding contributions and be sponsored by a parent or guardian if they are under 18 years old. So, for most parents and teachers who are still looking for a place where their kids and students can go to learn basic financial knowledge leading to action steps, KidsVest.org can be that place.

As previously suggested, wouldn't it be fantastic if kids could start initiating and contributing to their Roth IRA before they graduate high school? A significant number of kids, due to parental assistance, work enough hours to put $2,000-2,500 or more away per year for four years. Those kid's retirement portfolios can become $500,000-800,000 by age 60-65, simply because of the POWER OF TIME and COMPOUND INTEREST. And remember, the annual maximum Roth IRA contribution is $5,500. Bottom line, if your kids (alone or with your help) work and put more money in, they get more money out at retirement and most of these dollars will be tax free. In fact, the money kids put in their Roth IRA before age 20 may be more important than having parents pay their college educations.

Yet, we understand that a sum of $10,000, even over four years, is not possible for most American kids and families. It certainly would not have been possible for any of the Fouks kids. That's O.K.

Contributing early is more important than the actual dollar amount, since they have 40-45 years to save and invest.

A saying I like is "Investing small and soon beats large and later." You'll recall the table showing as much in the previous chapter. In the meantime, help your kid do the best they can in funding their Roth IRA. Whatever they or you help contribute, they will thank you later!

I also understand that it might take years of financial education for our kids to learn the mindset of working part or full-time and putting some money away during their youth. This is certainly true when kids have never been taught the importance of this goal. But with years of Kid$Vest financial health training, a much greater percentage of kids will finally "get it" and break this mold.

They will have learned to "pay themselves first" by making it a priority to put money into saving and investment accounts, before paying bills and expenses. Of course, this doesn't mean not paying bills because that would hurt their credit rating. It simply means that money is directly deposited into their savings and investment accounts. They won't see or miss it. As parents and teachers, the sooner we teach kids these lessons, the more positive the impact on their lives. Let's understand how the numbers can work.

A teen working 400 hours per year (33 hours per month) at $10 per hour will earn $4,000 per year. They can do yardwork, babysit/nanny or work at a job like McDonalds or Costco to earn this income. Not all kids can work during the school year at an outside job due to homework or extra-curricular activities. Perhaps they can work their 400 hours during the summer months (40 hrs. week X 10 weeks = 400 hours). Have your kids break the work hours out however it works best for them and your family.

Remember, we all have 24 hours a day X 365 days = 8,760 total hours per year. Discounting a third for sleep and we still have 5,782 hours. Don't you think financially educated kids can find 400 hours per year to lay the financial foundation for their entire life? I think they can too! It will obviously take knowledge, willpower and hard work to do it.

The above mentioned $4,000 earned could be broken down as follows:

Total Dollars Earned:	$4,000
Less: Taxes and Expenses	$ 500
Less: Roth IRA Contributions	$2,000-2,500
Remainder: Savings, Expenses and Fun	**$1,000-1,500**

Kids may work and earn more or fewer dollars than the example above, but whatever they contribute before they reach age twenty will be fantastic and will put them on the road to financial security. As important, we don't want them to wait to enjoy themselves along the way—that's why we put Fun in the remainder column.

If kids are really lucky, parents/grandparents funded a 529 Plan (dollars saved for college expenses) when they were born, and helped them fund their Roth IRA when they started working part or full-time. Or they matched some of their kid's savings and IRA contributions, as we noted in the previous action steps section. These fortunate kids can then move from basic financial security, the first and most important goal of Kid$Vest, to some serious wealth development. Finally, for those kids or families without means or work opportunities to initiate a Roth IRA, we will share our vision for the Kid$Vest Model below.

Before moving on, I have two qualifications about Kid$Vest.org that need mentioning.

1. An action step we previously mentioned but deserves highlighting, is kids ability to work. I believe parents must encourage their kids to work part or full-time during the year or in the summer, especially in their mid to late teens.

This is so vital to their financial well-being and personal development. Why? Learning the value of hard work is positive in its own right, but this is also how most kids can fund their Roth IRA and save for college. This is true even when parents can afford to pay their kid's expenses. We are not talking participation trophies here; we are talking *skin in the game.* So, we need kids to be taught the value of work again in America, and we need businesses to make it a priority to help them find part-time or summer jobs.

2. Kid$Vest.org isn't the only alternative that can offer kids financial education and action steps.

Kids and parents can also work with their individual brokers, financial advisors, and financial institutions to start their own investment programs and attain similar results. Kid$Vest truly wants all kids to be successful and how they access education and initiate investment is completely up to them and their parents. My only suggestion is that kids and parents start their financial program immediately. There is no time to waste—the compound interest train waits for no one!

The Kid$Vest.org organization and blog allow kids to access educational information and start action steps all in one place. That is our sole purpose for being! If that helps them stay focused and action-oriented, that is a win/win/win for participating kids, their families, and America. Besides, the investment fees charged by Kid$Vest's partners for setting up their retirement programs and index investment funds are some of the lowest in the industry. And lower fees mean higher returns!

In conclusion, the advantages of kids becoming Kid$Club Members, or simply applying our methodology on their own includes:

- Learning to live within their financial means by utilizing budgeting and savings skills that reduce debt and financial stress. Jean Chatzky, the financial editor for NBC's *Today Show*, confirms, "Debt really is trouble when it comes to people's financial and emotional lives."
- Watching their net worth and basic financial nest egg (Roth IRA) grow throughout their working life. The career and hobbies they choose as they age can then be pursued due to inspiration and desire, rather than being limited by the need for a paycheck from a job they have long outgrown. Most people over 50 years old know exactly what I'm talking about!
- Finally, with a substantial portfolio built up over forty or more years, they can comfortably do what they love during retirement. Why? Because they have saved and invested their way into an extended paycheck. Perhaps they can even pass on a small fortune to their families or worthy charities like

Kid$Vest.org so others have the same opportunity to achieve financial happiness!

The Kid$Vest Model–Coming to A Community Near You

The second approach to bringing financial education and actions steps to more American kids is by initiating the Kid$Vest Model in individual communities all over the U.S. This model, or platform can impact hundreds of thousands of American kids' lives. A simple example should show how the model works.

Let's say that Stillwater, MN, a community of 18,000 people, partners with Kid$Vest to initiate a Kid$Vest Model. The Stillwater community, at large, and District 834 believes that financial education and investment action is important to their approximately 8,500 students. First, Kid$Vest will help Stillwater identify and select 10-12 team leaders to manage the program. This Kid$Vest Committee (KVC) will include:

- School Board Chair (or liaison)
- School Superintendent
- Business teachers (2-3)
- Community business and financial leaders (2-4)
- Students (3-5): The day-to-day leaders of their Kid$Vest program

The Kid$Vest Committee is designed to coordinate the participation, engagement, and support from all important stakeholders in Stillwater. Without comprehensive backing from all these member groups, I would not suggest starting a Kid$Vest Program in your community. Too many obstacles must be overcome. Review **Chart 1** for The Kid$Vest Committee (KVC) Member Roles and Responsibilities.

	SUPPORT KV PROJECT	K-12 CURRICULUM	LEAD AND MANAGE PROJECT	SUMMER JOBS AND FUNDING	MARKETING PROGRAM	DISTRIBUTE FUNDS	BACK OFFICE PARTNER
SCHOOL ADMINISTRATION AND BOARD	X	X					
TEACHERS	X	X	X				
STUDENTS	X	X	X	X	X	X	
BUSINESS LEADERS	X			X	X		
Kid$Vest	X	X	X	X	X	X	X
	THE Kid$Vest MODEL						

Chart 1

Second, the KVC, with Kid$Vest's assistance, will make decisions concerning financial curriculum sources and modules, as well as teacher education.

Third, all district students automatically become Kid$Club Members with access to financial education in the classroom and through the Kid$Vest website. Students can now learn how to budget, save, and invest. The *Kid$Vest Financial Binder* (Addendum 1) will be an additional resource all kids can use to strategically plan their future. They can also use their Kid$Club memberships to take financial action by setting up their very first Roth IRA. Kid$Vest financial partners (to be named later) will handle all the back-office IRA applications, provide numerous low-cost investment funds and forward quarterly statements to students.

We hope kids contribute up to $2000-2500 per year for four years as we previously discussed, but anything they can afford still puts them on the road to financial security. I believe over time 40-60% of Stillwater's students will take advantage of the program and many will put meaningful dollars in their Roth IRA. Why not? The cost to join is—Free.

Fourth, and a highlight of the Kid$Vest Model, would be to enlist the support of the local financial community to offer loans to kids who don't have the financial means to fund their own Roth IRA. As you recall, the last of our core goals of Kid$Vest is "To make sure kids and parents without means are included in the strategy."

What if disadvantaged kids had access to local banks or credit unions through the Kid$Vest Model and could take out a reduced interest loan between $2,500-8,000, or whatever they could afford, during their four high school years? Their Roth IRA is funded, and perhaps an emergency or savings account is initiated as well. Of course, kids must have a part or full-time job to pay off the loan before they graduate.

Don't tune out yet, because I know what you're thinking! *The Kid$Vest Project* is all about understanding BSI techniques, while being careful of debt. So why am I suggesting that kids, especially disadvantaged kids, take out a loan to fund their Roth IRA? On the surface, that sounds counter-intuitive, if not idiotic. Again, it comes back to compound interest, the fuel for the financial success we discussed in Chapter 1. If there is no other way a kid can fund a Roth IRA without a loan, then I would support them doing so—if they are working. This expense must be dealt with during their personal budget process.

If we have taught kids well in the classroom or on our website, financially educated kids can hopefully make sound decisions. And remember, I'm suggesting that whatever they borrow, they pay off before they graduate high school. After that, they will likely start accumulating larger expenses like car or college loans. Funding an early Roth IRA with as many dollars as they can spare, still puts them further ahead than peers who start their Roths IRAs or 401(k) plans when they are 25 or 30 years old. We showed as much in previous compound interest examples. Delayed gratification is a bummer, isn't it?

Now, why will local banks and credit unions be interested in offering low interest loans to Kid$Club Members? Because:

- Helping disadvantaged kids in their community is the right thing to do
- Assisting approximately 10-20% of Stillwater's high school kids with loans of between $2,500-

8,000 over four years should mean thousands of dollars in fees
- Finally, there is minimal risk of default if the loan is guaranteed

Yes, you heard that right, the loans can be guaranteed. The coup de gras of the model would be for the KVC business members to source community dollars and initiate a *Financial Literacy Fund*. This money could be used for the program's minimal expenses, but also to guarantee the bank loans of member kids. Banks and credit unions are guaranteed they won't lose money on Kid$Vest loans. A deal they shouldn't refuse!

To continue our example, let's say the Stillwater's business community comes up with $100,000 in the Financial Literacy Fund over several years. Perhaps successful business owners or philanthropists could be partners or sponsors of this fund. The Kid$Vest Model may not be able to help disadvantaged kids afford full funding of their Roth IRA, but kids can certainly take advantage of the financial education and some funding.

Once the community donors and school district relationships are established, Kid$Vest and the student members of the KVC will help market the program to individual students and the community. Together we will put on presentations and work within the community to market the Model so everyone understands the program's goals and structure.

The KVC and Kid$Vest will administer and moderate the program in the following ways:

- Coordinate the program with the school system, teachers, local business leaders, and kids to make sure the program is successful and marketed to the benefit of all students.
- Offer curriculum assistance from Kid$Vest modules, or other free educational modules, developed by organizations like CEE and NEFE.
- Develop teacher education as well as classroom training and/or the use of the Kid$Vest website.
- Kid$Vest and partners will handle all Kid$Club member applications and signups, as well as back office Roth IRA administration work to ensure the success of the program.

As kids from all grades take advantage of financial education in the classroom and on-line, teens who work (typically students 13-18 years old) can then initiate Roth IRAs and start funding them. As we suggested, all students in the Stillwater community will become Kid$Club Members.

In summary, all Stillwater students would now be part of a financial program that could change their lives forever. We do understand that not all of them will take advantage of the Kid$Vest Model; some will not be interested or meet the IRS work requirements. You can only help those kids, or communities for that matter, who want to be helped!

Let's dream of what a successful program can do for the Stillwater community. First, gone is the lack of financial health training for all students. They will pick up valuable BSI tips, even if only by osmosis. Second, anyone who sets up a Roth IRA and participates over the four or more years will likely have the beginnings of a terrific retirement portfolio. We are hopeful that at least 40-60% of the students will initiate Roth IRAs over time and contribute at least a modest dollar amount. Baby steps for America, we know, but we must start somewhere!

Many of Stillwater's students' lives (or the lives of your community's students) and careers will be changed for the better! Consider how many of these kids will have a fighting chance at financial security. Perhaps some of them will start businesses that rejuvenate the community and add tax revenues. All because they have learned and applied their financial knowledge.

> **(Please note that the Stillwater School District and community have not initiated *The Kid$Vest Model.* This beautiful, suburban Minnesota St. Croix River City is only used as an example because it is the birthplace of Minnesota and my hometown. Go Ponies!)**

Now imagine this same scenario being played out in numerous communities all over America, where too many kids are accumulating debt and not initiating Roth IRAs. Communities where kids have no reason to finish high school or stay and live in places with little growth potential. What if people like Warren Buffet, Bill Gates and other wealthy individuals offer Financial Literacy Fund dollars, not just to a specific community, but to kids who apply for local loans on a national scale.

Now we begin to change America at the grass roots level—the ultimate impetus for initiating Kid$Vest.org. But for now, we need to walk before we can run! As more and more communities begin to participate, America starts growing a middle class with power—financial power. That's what our model is intended to do!

In the end, the Kid$Vest Model goal is to make certain every child who is willing to learn, work, save, and invest, becomes financially successful in life. We will measure Kid$Vest's success by the number of kids who take advantage of our school curriculum and website, and how many Roth IRAs are initiated. Below are two examples of smart, motivated kids who I read about and are already taking charge of their financial lives.

Hillary Lutkus is a 13-year-old Denver resident who, due to the education and mentoring of her mother, started a dog-walking business. After her company had earned more than $2,000, she started investing in CDs and is beginning to add mutual funds. At a young age, she has budgeting, saving, and investing skills that should carry her to financial independence throughout her entire life. Now if she started a Roth IRA when she turned 15-16, we would really be impressed.

Damon Williams, by age 14, "has built a portfolio worth $50,000, knows blue chips like most kids know potato chips, and saves more than he spends." At age five, with undoubtedly solid parental guidance, this Chicago native bought his first share of Nike stock and continued to invest his Christmas cash in other equities. As he has grown, he continues to learn about living within his means and how compound interest works in his favor over time. These kids and their parents make us all proud!

We want millions of kids like Hillary and Damon using financial knowledge and acting out their dreams in America! Educating our kids at home and then in the classroom is critically important in changing attitudes and helping them make better money choices.

Finally, let's not forget about businesses across America. What if Kid$Vest educational seminars or workshops were provided to company employees and employees' kids as a benefit to the organization? Hundreds, maybe thousands, of parents can lead their children into a world of financial freedom because they will understand BSI techniques. Hey, corporate America, let's get involved for the financial benefit of your employees and their kids!

The Kid$Vest Model can have major benefits for our kids and young adults across America. "Let the games begin!"

"At first dreams seem impossible, then improbable, then inevitable."

Christopher Reeve

Chapter

FOUR

THE DREAMLIFE PYRAPUZZLE

As previously mentioned, I loved basketball as a kid. So when my dad, a successful basketball and football coach at Hudson High School, showed me John Wooden's basketball Pyramid for Success, I kept a printed copy of it in my bedroom. Wooden, the renowned UCLA basketball coach (1948-1975), is still regarded as perhaps the best basketball coach of all time. Wooden's Bruins won a record ten national championships and had star players like Kareem Abdul-Jabbar, Bill Walton, Gail Goodrich, and Lucius Allen, to name a few. Mr. Wooden, known as the Wizard of Westwood, was legendary for teaching and coaching young players at the highest level. As importantly, he prepared them for life!

The attached Wooden Pyramid of Success **(Chart 2)** has fifteen traits such as loyalty, poise, confidence, team spirit, conditioning, and competitive greatness, which all his players had to learn and emulate. It showed what he expected of them as players and as men. And more importantly, what they should expect of themselves.

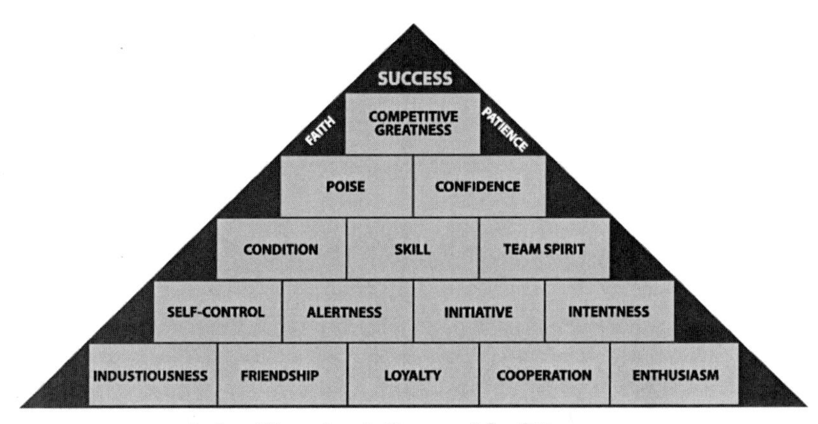

John Wooden's Pyramid of Success

Chart 2, John Wooden's Pyramid of Success

Later, at Stillwater High School in Minnesota, my social studies teacher brought out Maslow's Needs Hierarchy, shown in **Chart 3**. Abraham Maslow, the American psychologist, rated a man's needs on five levels going from basic biological and physiological needs such as food, water, warmth, sex, and sleep to self-actualization.

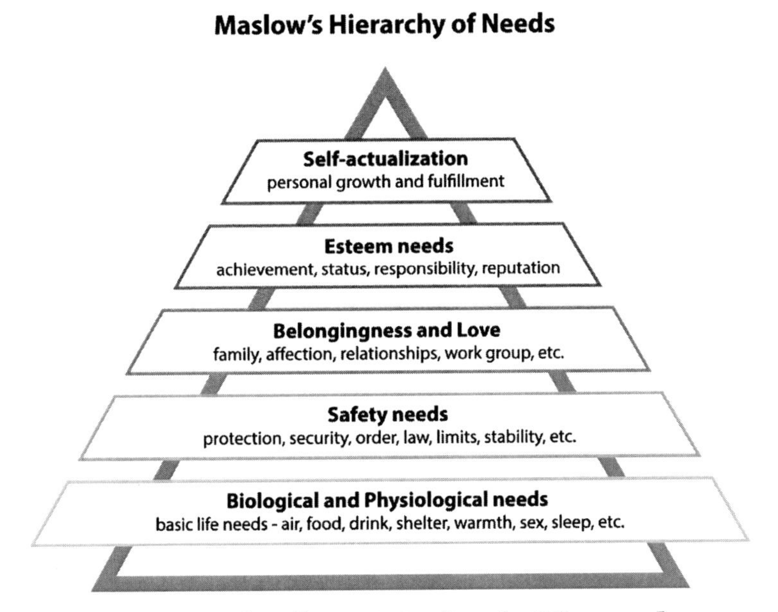

Chart 3, Abraham Maslow's Hierarchy of Needs

Both the Maslow and Wooden pyramids had a huge effect on me (visual learner that I am). During a 40-year career in management and leadership roles, I developed my own "Pyramid on Leadership." I use it personally, and I also used it with the training classes I taught over the years.

More recently, with my passion to have our youth become functional in BSI techniques, I developed the Kid$Vest DreamLife PyraPuzzle **(Chart 4)**. It shares the fundamental building blocks of financial knowledge that can lead anyone to financial security. I believe it could be a working outline or the foundation for future financial health curriculum at home and within our educational systems. We learned in previous chapters how desperately this is needed. At the very least, it would be a great starting point for parents and teachers regarding the financial education of our youth!

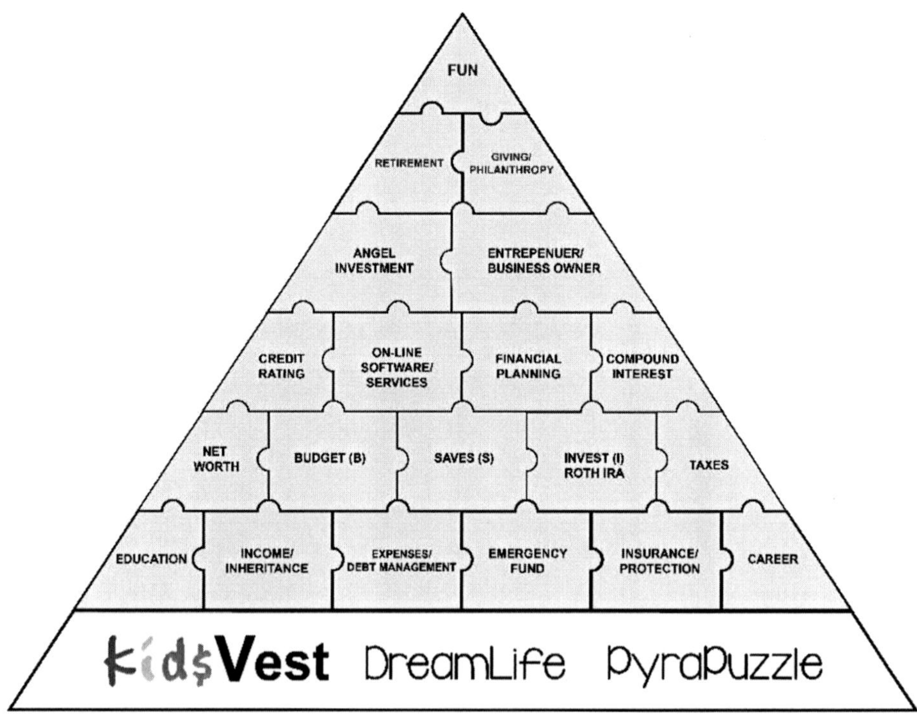

Chart 4, Kid$Vest DreamLife PyraPuzzle

©DreamLife PyraPuzzle by GregAFouks 2016

As you view it, you'll notice the shape is pyramidal. It shows basic educational needs at the foundation, financial tools in the middle and then a pinnacle like Maslow's self-actualization level. But its pieces also interconnect like a puzzle. The message of these interconnected shapes is that these skills need to be learned, practiced, and applied to financial situations as needed. At times, we may be more worried about BSI principles, while at other times we are thinking about an entrepreneurial idea or simply want to do something for fun. You can't master one skill and go onto the next level like Maslow's hierarchy. No, you may need to access specific financial skills, at a moment's notice, to take advantage of a financial opportunity or challenge ahead of you. Why do you think financial literacy is so hard to obtain and maintain?

Each kid's individual DreamLife will naturally be different than their parents, peers, or friends. Or as Tim Cook, Apple CEO, would say, "Let your joy be in your journey—not in some distant goal." For instance, individuals can become an entrepreneur at any age—as soon as they perceive a need and offer a solution to the problem. What if Bill Gates and Paul Allen had waited or hesitated in their software development business because they thought they needed more experience? Microsoft might be in a very different evolutionary spot today!

The remainder of this chapter will highlight each of the DreamLife PyraPuzzle modules individually. All of them are extremely important to a kid's overall financial success and should be incorporated into their personal DreamLife strategic plan at the appropriate time. That is, parents and teachers might play games, or have scheduled discussions around the dinner table, or in the classroom about each of these modules. Remember those actions steps we noted in the last chapter.

We want your kids to start becoming financially educated on all the topics before they need them. Some of these topics, like income and taxes, are simple concepts that parents and teachers already understand and personally use each day. We want your kids to learn each of them individually and how they work together to afford them their own DreamLife. That is how they gain financial security while having fun along the way. Some of the modules require only a short definition as they are recognizable concepts, while others will be detailed in future chapters.

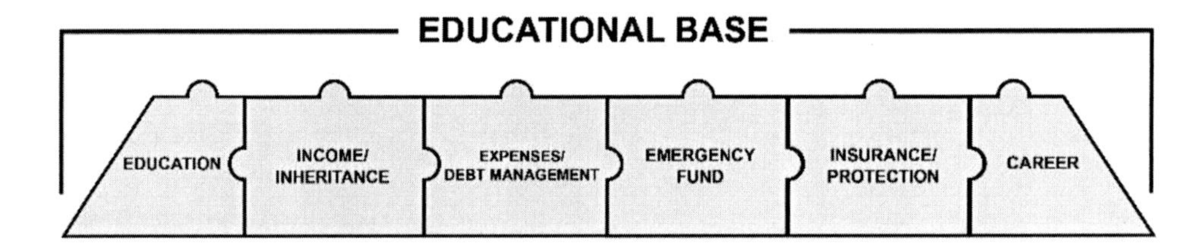

EDUCATION:

Although it's shocking, only 80% of our high school kids graduate, with three of five minority students not finishing the 12th grade. Fortunately, many do return to pass their GED high school equivalency exam. Also, depending on which survey you look at, between 60-70% of students who finish high school enroll in college. Only 56% of those individuals go on to graduate. The income and career statistics are undeniable regarding the substantial income differential between those who are educated beyond the high school and college level.

The median household income for college graduates is $78,200, but those households headed with high school diplomas only earned $36,700. The Pew Research Center estimates that after factoring in the costs of college along with the diminished earnings during an individual's work life, the typical college graduate earns $550,000 more than the typical high school graduate over a lifetime. Furthermore, unemployment rates for college graduates are half of what they are for people who have only high school diplomas.

Table 2 shows more detailed information regarding the value of education considering income and net worth accumulation.

Education level	Median income	Median net worth
No high school diploma	$22,200	$33,200
High school diploma only	$36,700	$80,300
Some college	$45,600	$84,700
College degree	$78,200	$280,800

Table 2

However, and this is a key fundamental of The DreamLife PyraPuzzle, we are not telling you that a successful life, career or financial independence can be obtained only if our kids collect a college or graduate degree. While I am always in favor of kids going on to college for the education and the socialization experiences they gain, college isn't right or needed by everyone.

In the movie, *Nobody's Fool,* Paul Newman talks to his son about the six months, years ago, this "Jack of all trades" had spent attending college. He told his son, "I was good at it." When his son asked why he didn't stay or graduate, Newman responded, "I said I was good at it, I didn't say that I belonged there." Kids who have already started businesses, attend trades schools, or simply go directly into the workforce can certainly be wildly successful. Not everyone belongs in college. Bill Gates hasn't done too badly!

Of course, as the above table shows, advanced education certainly can give your kid a leg up monetarily towards their financial and career goals, so don't be dismissive of its benefits. But education alone doesn't necessarily guarantee success. So encourage your kids to go to college if they need it to achieve their personal goals, especially if you offer them financial assistance. Or, have them consider a gap year (or years) to determine what they are good at and what they want, especially if they desire to fund their Roth IRA, travel, or save for college. It's not a bad alternative!

Financial Education:

I would certainly be remiss if I didn't mention financial education as part of kids overall learning life. I can guarantee financial independence if the Kid$Vest principles of financial education and action steps are implemented. This is true no matter what career your kid chooses. It comes down to what Suzy Orman says, "Living below your means so you can live above your needs." Obviously, our kid's life style will be dramatically different if they become a rock star, rather than a teacher. But they can obtain financial independence, give back and have fun along the way in almost any career!

INCOME:

Income is the gross dollar amount earned each week or month. This is the total cash inflow kids must budget, save, and invest. I would strongly suggest they set goals in this area as they progress through their career, as only earning a minimum wage will make it harder to financially succeed. While higher income careers are important to some people, merely having a high income doesn't necessarily equal financial security or happiness. It is what you do with what you earn that is of the utmost importance.

EXPENSES / DEBT MANAGEMENT:

Monthly bills your kids pay on time will help them establish a good credit rating. This could include rent, living expenses, car payments, and health insurance. How kids manage their expenses throughout their life will be very important to their overall financial security.

Debt management is also important to their financial success. How they handle big debts such as college (if they attend), cars, and housing can directly affect their happiness quotient. We have devoted an entire chapter towards this topic in Chapter 5—Life's Big Financial Moments.

EMERGENCY FUND:

You never know when extra funds might be needed. Therefore, it is important to have a three to six-month emergency fund available for unforeseen expenses. Not all emergencies are necessarily tragic or devastating to a kid's financial well-being. But most of them must be addressed immediately to avoid larger financial or future health problems. Some of these can include: car repairs, accidents, or even toothaches. They often come up unexpectedly and can blow your monthly budget/savings plan. So set aside a certain amount of income each month to prepare for these surprises. Of course, some surprises may be very positive, like taking advantage of a business opportunity during a financial downturn in real estate, low stock prices, or a fire sale on a new car. If they have these funds set aside, they can access them as needed. Just make sure they replenish the emergency fund for any future needs.

In their teens and early twenties, I suggest kids spend less time worrying about their emergency fund and more time on funding their Roth IRA (at least up to $10,000). This is because our basic premise of investing in their future is to take advantage of compound interest. Whether it is your kid, or you who makes their first Roth IRA contributions, that should be your priority during these years. This is so important to their financial future!

Once their Roth IRA is funded, then they can start saving for emergency, savings, or investment funds, whichever is a priority at the time. Job loss is one setback many people face at one time or another. Establishing an emergency fund will help overcome such losses throughout their working life. It can be financially devastating if they are not prepared to be out of work for a time. You want your kids to be able to confront emergencies or opportunities as they arise and their emergency fund will offer them this advantage.

Since these thoughts may be somewhat controversial, read what other financial experts say and decide for yourself. I believe my approach is effective because when your kids are young, you might be able to help them with healthcare, housing, car expenses, or other financial emergencies. Their emergency expenses will probably be more manageable when they are living at home. Most likely this will change when they get older, move away from home, marry, start a family, and are well into a career.

INSURANCE / PROTECTION:

As soon as they can, and certainly when they are on a wealth building plan in their twenties, you want their assets protected. Life insurance, health insurance, and disability coverage are the most important three, along with the emergency fund described above. Luckily, most young people are still covered by their parents plans until age 23-26 or can get by with very low-cost insurance coverage. As they start their career, hopefully, their employer will offer basic life insurance, health care, and disability coverages they can opt into. Finally, home insurance (for the house and its contents) and car insurance are often mandatory in most states, should they own a home or auto.

Since I have my CLU, and worked in the insurance field early in my career, I offer these comments about term vs. whole life coverage. Term life is initially inexpensive and offers simple protection. Only pay for the protection needed early in life (between $100,000-200,000), but don't go overboard on the coverage and compromise your savings and investments. Whole life insurance is more expensive early on but can be a forced savings vehicle if your kids are savings procrastinators. However, it is not cheap. I recommend getting cost effective protection with term life in their twenties and adding some whole life insurance later, if possible. This will depend on their budget and health at the time. Ask an expert, such as a CPA, JD, or financial planner for recommendations and help to understand their own personal needs.

CAREER:

Your kid may want to be a fireman, coach, mechanical engineer, or entrepreneur. Their ultimate career choice will certainly have a huge impact on the kind of lifestyle they live. There are a fortunate few who grow up wanting to be doctors and then have the required motivation and intelligence to follow that dream. Most of us, however, go to high school, college, or enter the workforce without knowing our specific long-term goals. This is not a problem. As we work and learn, we often change our minds about our careers or fall into a career by chance.

For example, some kids may want to be physicians and then change their mind when they learn they can't stand the sight of blood or can't get into medical school. Poor eyesight might mean their desire to pilot jets isn't in the cards. Or they might go to trade school to be a plumber, then later start their own residential real estate company. It is very difficult to plan anyone's exact future until experience or luck brings them into a career they hopefully are meant for.

In the movie, *The Rookie,* Jim Morris' father told his talented baseball player son that "It is OK to do what you want to do when you are young, until it is time to do what you were meant to do." Jim Morris Jr. tried out for the Major Leagues at age 30, despite his father's discouraging words. He became a relief pitcher for the Tampa Bay Rays for two seasons. Miracles do happen!

As someone who worked as an executive search recruiter for fifteen years and hired thousands of employees from the front line to the C-suite (CEO, CFO etc.), I have often been asked to talks to kids looking for jobs or just beginning their careers. I came up with seven steps to Finding a Position, which can be especially helpful early in one's career. The steps include:

- Know Thyself (Socrates)
- What is your passion
- What industries do you like
- What specific companies appeal to you
- What kind of leader will you be working for
- Just get a job—any damn job

- Job offer negotiation knowledge

Know Thyself:

It is critically important that your kid understands what makes him/her tick. Do they have some natural leadership skills like vision or strategy? Are they good project managers? Is math their thing, or are they more artistic in nature? Are they good at building things or at creative writing?

I believe that we are all given strengths or gifts that set us apart from our family, friends, peers and fellow employees.

I learned two very important truths in the executive search business. One, "No one gets the whole package," so make sure your kids pay attention to their gifts and get connected to careers that fit them well. And two, "There is always someone better than you," so deal with it!

If your kid can't write down her major talents on a single sheet of paper, or they aren't sure they are accurate in their assessments, there are numerous assessment tools that can be of assistance. For instance, the old Myers-Briggs tests, StrengthsFinder, or Profile XT assessments are all helpful. They all offer insights into your best personality traits. There are also numerous life coaches in every community who can interview and test your kids to uncover their personal gifts. Finally, Addendum 1, Section 1 (My 3 Year Personal Assessment & Financial Goals) of *The Kid$Vest Financial Binder* offers a quick assessment of strengths, gifts, passions, and financial goals. This can be completed annually to keep them on track.

Personal Passions:

Once they know themselves – their likes, dislikes, and interests, then try to help them find a career that revolves around their passions. Mark Zuckerberg of Facebook noted, "If you just work on stuff that you like and you're passionate about, you don't have to have a master plan with how things will play out." Or, as I have often been told, "when you do what you love, you end up loving what you do."

On the other hand, financial literacy author Marty Nemko says, that "We have all been sold a bill of goods when we are told to follow our passions, or do what you love and the money will follow. Yes, some people do what they love, and the money follows. Others make less money but still are happy, but millions have followed their passion and still haven't earned enough money to pay back their student loans, let alone make a middle-class living doing what they are passionate about."

So first see if they can find a position that fits their current passions and gifts. However, if nothing is available in those areas, have them move forward. Only the lucky few find their passion or gifts fit their first job right out of the box. While they are learning about their individual skills and desires, have them start planning for what might be their ultimate *dream job*. If it never occurs and they end up in a career that satisfies them or at least covers their needs, they can always get involved in their passion as a hobby or give back philanthropically. Most people would kill to have either one of these options available to them during their career.

Industry Likes:

If your kid can't find their initial career involving their direct passion, then help them look at industries in your community that might fit their background. For example, healthcare is big in the Twin Cities of Minneapolis and St. Paul, where I live. Industry giants like 3M, Medtronic, and United Healthcare, along with hundreds of medical device manufacturers, all are headquartered here.

Specific Companies:

If specific industries in your area aren't hiring, then have your kids list approximately twenty-five small or large local companies in any industry that they admire or hear good things about. Networking with friends and relatives who work at these companies or know people who do, and asking them for help regarding openings that fit their skill set is smart. That is the way many jobs are filled today. Have them keep companies on their radar and review open positions monthly or quarterly to see if any openings sound good to them. If so, they can apply, but see if they can find a reference to help them navigate the hiring process.

Your kids may not want to hear this, but getting a job is still about who you know, not what you know, especially early in their career. The older or more experienced they become, the more they will agree with this truth. For instance, my daughter recently moved back to the Twin Cities and was looking for a new position. She ran into a former friend at a gathering, who just happened to be in HR at a large Minneapolis company. Her evening of fun networked into a contact and future interview with this company. As it turned out, she got the job. She still had to use her talents, knowledge and skill to get hired, but she got her foot in the door. You must first get a foot in the door before you can knock it down.

Respected Boss:

Your kid's first job offer might come from a company that may not have been at the top of their industry or company list. Yet it might be a position where they can gain experience and earn a reasonable income. In this case, make sure that their boss is highly respected by her team. How do they find this out? They can ask pertinent questions of their future boss and her team during the interview process. They will learn twice as much, and have many more internal growth opportunities by working for a talented, successful person. In any job, industry, or company this will be important, but especially at companies farther down on their passion or industry list. It's likely they won't stay in this position for long, but they don't want to just kill time working for an unproductive or poor leader.

Take Any Damn Job:

Finally, if your kid has worked the previous steps and have still not found a position, have them keep applying like mad and take the best available job. Maybe it's the only job available at the time. They shouldn't despair. As we suggested before, early in their career they may be unsure as to their path or gifts. Or a recession may cause jobs to be scarce in a field they would choose. Tell them to find a job and just start working! They will learn what they like, and don't like, and can pay bills or fund their retirement account in the meantime.

Companies often hire people with experience, any experience, so any job is better than no job. Even a so-so position might set them on the path for a great second or third position. There are numerous job self-help books out there such as *Moving the Needle: Get Clear, Get Free and Get Going in Your Career, Business and Life* by Joe Sweeney, *What Color Is Your Parachute* by Richard Bolles, *Getting from College to Career: Your Essential Guide to Succeeding in the Real World* by Lindsey Pollak, or *The Career Chronicles* by Michael Gregory, which can be of assistance.

Compensation Negotiation:

Once they go through the interview process and a company likes them, the next step is a written offer. This assumes they are applying for a true career position, not simply a minimum wage job. With a written offer, they might be able to negotiate a few things. The position and/or title could be negotiable. If this is an entry level position, that may be unlikely. Most important is the compensation for the position. I always try to look at the Total Compensation package before deciding if the offer is a good one or not.

For example, total compensation can include base salary, bonus or commission, benefits like a matching 401(k) plan, vacation or PTO time, health and disability benefits, and other perks. Other things might include tuition reimbursement, free parking, gym memberships, or complimentary lunches, etc. If the company wants them badly, or this is more than an entry level position, they should be able to negotiate some things. Always remember, "In basketball, the shots you don't take don't go in." Not asking for additional compensation or benefits is the same as expecting to score without taking a shot. Besides, what can asking hurt? One company's base salary might be less, but the hours, free parking, or bonuses offered could make up this difference in a hurry. Perhaps one job offers you a ten minute commute or is close to a trout stream you like to visit. All factors should be taken into consideration. Have them ask for the most they can in total compensation—if they are professional with their questions, the worst that can happen is to be told no.

The main rule of compensation negotiation is—he who speaks numbers first usually loses! When a company wants to hire your kid, typically the hiring manager, or HR person, will ask them what they want to earn, or what they have been earning. Their response should always be, "what is the range of the position?" Let me say this again. "What is the range of the position?" They will either answer their question or try again to get them to name their price. Once they understand the range, always suggest that they should be at the top of the range.

Why? Because they should value themselves. Their skills and work ethic will allow them to successfully perform the job. They may disagree with this assessment and suggest they can go no higher than X-dollars, but at least they have a starting point. Once a specific offer is made, your kid should look down with a slight frown on their face (even if they are ecstatic about the offer) and say nothing until the other person speaks first. Seeing their disappointment and knowing they want your kid at the company could get them some additional compensation. At the very least, hopefully, they might ask what your kid is thinking. They could then say they were expecting slightly more compensation, bonus or vacation days. Low and behold, they may get more! Your kid might not be comfortable with this kind of negotiation, but it has proven successful.

Asking these questions and looking down without speaking first could earn them thousands of dollars more to start in a job. If they ask for and receive $1,000-2,000 more to start, or after a promotion, these additional dollars will set the tone of a higher base for the rest of their life. This is like compound interest on their investments, so have them pay attention! Over the course of their career, these simple negotiation techniques could earn them tens of thousands of dollars more—simply because they knew how to negotiate and ask for what they want!

For example, my spouse was interviewing for a medical sales job when we moved back to the Twin Cities from Washington D.C. Her previous medical and sales background allowed her to get an offer from a small start-up medical laboratory. She wanted the job, and they wanted her, so they started negotiating the salary and bonus for the position. I suggested she use the same techniques I mentioned—asking about the salary and bonus potential.

As you might expect, if you have a higher base your bonus potential might be somewhat less and vice versa. As they were negotiating, the owner threw up her hands and said, "I hate negotiations, how about if you work hard and we give you both the higher base and bonus?" My wife was astounded but hastily agreed. Stories like this don't happen often, so she was very fortunate. But some negotiation knowledge led to a win-win for both my wife and the owner, as she worked for the organization for over fifteen years. They were both successful and remain friends today. So ask the questions and don't be embarrassed.

In fact, Penelope Wang for *Money*, recently asked several Millennials what the biggest financial mistake they had made to date. Two of her respondents, Stephen Valdivia from the University of Florida and Megan Leonhardt of Ohio University, both said they didn't negotiate hard enough for higher salaries on their first jobs. They said they regretted not doing a good job on researching their positions or valuing themselves. This cost them significant dollars up front, and perhaps a great deal more over their careers. So have your kids be bold, but professional, when compensation negotiation occurs—ultimately it is your kid's career and their responsibility.

Finally, if your kid is one of the lucky potential new employees who has multiple job offers, have them use these negotiating techniques to get the very best offer possible. I would suggest not playing one company against the other for their services, as they will come off looking egotistical and unprofessional. But they should negotiate the best offer they can and lay the offers side by side when making their decision. Remember, the best offer is not always the one that pays the most.

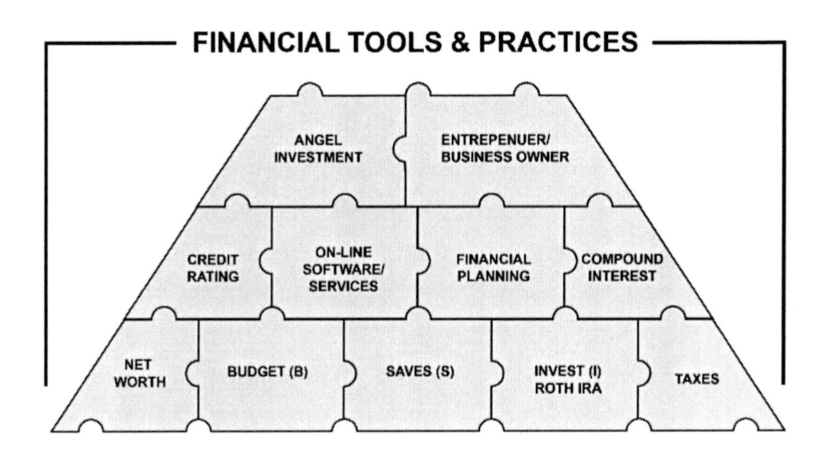

NET WORTH:

These next six Financial Tools in the PyraPuzzle of net worth, budgeting, saving, investing, taxes, and credit rating will form the basis for what I call the *Kid$Vest Financial Binder* or Financial Strategic Plan (Addendum 1). These factors are extremely important to your kid's financial success. They should either be tracked electronically or on simple sheets of paper, or both. They should monitor them quarterly, or annually, for best results.

The section of your *Financial Binder*, after Personal Assessment and Master Vendor List, is net worth. A net worth statement simply shows all their assets, minus their debts/liabilities, with the difference being their net worth or equity. This is how they keep score of their overall success. While their personal net worth will likely be low or negative until they are in their mid-twenties or later, watching and adjusting their progress along life's journey is very smart. I personally have kept an annual net worth page since I was 30 years old. I know, I should have been keeping track sooner, but no one taught me the Kid$Vest philosophy. Over the years, it has been fun watching my family's assets grow, while our debts decreased. We continuously monitor the progress we are making toward our personal financial security, and your kid should do so as well.

BUDGET (B):

Next in the Financial Tools and Practices section of the PyraPuzzle is BSI and Taxes. Together they form the heart of *The Kid$Vest Project* and the guts of your *Financial Binder*. If your kid understands and applies these tools properly early in their career, it really will be hard to mess up having a financially secure life. I personally use simple written forms for each one of these tools, because I am an old guy. However, I also keep electronic files from numerous apps, as millennials are likely to do. Both are acceptable, just make sure they do something! Some well-known electronic apps include Mint, PersonalCapital, or PowerWallet, etc.

Budgeting is the process that adds up what income they bring in monthly, then subtracts their expenses and taxes from the total. Simply put, cash inflow versus cash outflows. A budget helps them plan how to spend or save their income and can also track their actual spending habits. Utilized properly, this tool can become one of their greatest weapons for financial security. Once a budget is implemented, their goal is to break even or have a positive remainder. Remainders are discretionary items—*gifts from the gods* that we can put toward emergency expenses, savings, investments, or even vacations! **Addendum 2** shows a sample Budget or Spending Plan.

Paying yourself first is critical for the success of The Kid$Vest Project. Remember, this means you set aside money for savings, emergency funds, and investments as a priority before expenses, needs, and wants. As we said before, if putting away 10-20% of their income isn't possible, they can start out by doing 2-3%, or whatever they can spare. Just make sure the dollars they put away are meaningful and that they continue to raise the percentage as their income and needs allow.

After taxes (which you must pay) they should be building a personal savings and investment plan, as well as initiating their Roth IRA. Remember, these early savings and investments ultimately become their wealth building machine throughout their life, while the Roth IRA or 401(k) become their retirement "pot of gold." This is primarily due to the compound interest accumulation we discussed earlier.

Once your kid is in the workforce, they should immediately begin contributing to their company's 401K and/or an individual IRA. This should be done in conjunction with their emergency fund and saving goals.

SAVE (S):

Once you offer your kid an allowance, or they have a trust fund, or are gainfully employed and receive a monthly income, they must decide where best to allocate their funds. Before they spend a dime of their net income (after taxes), they should save at least 10-20% (or as we said above, as much as they can) of their total income. A portion of these dollars can then go into their emergency fund, a goal account, or into retirement savings. It all depends on their prioritized needs at the time. Then they can use the remainder for life's expenses—their needs and wants. This simple concept is critical to becoming financially secure now, and as they age.

One trick I was taught by my first boss was to save your first raise and continue doing so throughout your career. For example, let's say your starting salary is $45,000 at your first job. In year two, you get a 2.5% raise and are then earning approximately $46,125. Take that additional $1,125 (less after taxes) and direct deposit the money into your existing saving account. Essentially, you are still living at your first paycheck level. If they can stay one raise behind for life, they will build up a nice windfall in time. This really works well when they get a significant promotion and their salary jumps quickly.

INVEST (I):

Part of what your kid saves monthly should go into investments. This may include 401(k) or IRAs dollars, but once they exceed the companies match (if they offer one), some of their savings should go into an investment account. How these two accounts are separated into their own pools, depends on one's specific income and expenses. I don't want them putting all their investing dollars into their retirement account because they may need some of these dollars for expenses, debts, real estate, a home, fun and the stock market. Yes, the stock market!

If your kids are not participating in the growth of the US economy, it is very difficult for the average American to become wealthy or financially secure. Oh, your kid could win the lottery or become a successful entrepreneur or business owner. But many business owners and entrepreneurs don't make it (80%). This isn't often discussed in the media, but it's is true.

Putting all their eggs in one basket can be a smart move at times, but not for your entire lifetime. That is too risky! For example, Bill Gates, Steve Jobs and Mark Zuckerberg had their personal incomes tied to their companies early in their lives. They took calculated risks and won the game! But not all business owners or entrepreneurs succeed, especially at that impressive level. We all must have fallback careers and investment programs in place.

Of course IRAs or 401(k)s are typically invested in mutual funds or ETFs, but these funds are tied up until retirement and touching them is generally a bad idea. The penalties and taxes for accessing these funds early can be devastating to your kid's future retirement goals.

Read famed TV investment guru Jim Cramer's books on investing, or one of the hundreds of the other financial guru books (such as *Rich Dad Poor Dad* by

Robert Kiyosaki) if they want to learn how to successfully beat the market, or understand product minefields. For our purposes, we want things simple at first so they can experiment later when they have the time and interest to trade at their own discretion.

For the Roth IRA we hope kids initiate in their late teens, putting this money in a low-cost index fund is totally appropriate. Both investor Warren Buffet and Jack Bogle (Vanguard Group founder) support this idea. The magic of compounding interest and lower fund fees will make their investment returns the best they can be. Jim Cramer recently said, "A 22-year-old with $10,000 invested for 40 years earns about $450,000 for the investor. Sounds vaguely familiar, doesn't it? And if kids practice *The Kid$Vest Project* and start saving in their late teens, then add more 401(k) dollars throughout their life, they can dollar cost average their way to even more significant wealth. For instance, the $450,000 mentioned above can be substantially higher.

TAXES:

For each dollar earned, Uncle Sam will always take a piece of the action. We can all complain about how this money is being spent, but the fact is we all must deduct this from our income during the year, especially if we don't look good in stripes or want to end up behind bars. Ask actors Wesley Snipes, Willie Nelson or Nicholas Cage about their past IRS struggles. Always plan for taxes right away and have the proper amount taken out of your paycheck monthly.

Kids' tax bills will depend on their income and deductions. The more adjusted gross income they earn, the higher their tax bracket will be, and the higher the percentage of their income will be taxed. In the United States this is called a progressive tax. Capital gains income or dividends must be included in one's overall income, but they typically have lower tax rates. Also, try to help your kids find ways to legally reduce their tax bills by using deductions and credits. That is unless they are better off simply using the standard deduction. They typically don't earn much from summer jobs so we want them to keep most of what they earn. I personally hope we radically change and simplify our tax system, as so many politicians are advocating.

An example of a tax credit some kids can utilize is the *Savers Tax Credit*. It was designed to help lower-income families contribute to retirement plans. If your kid qualifies, this credit essentially pays them to put money in their retirement account. They can write off the first $2,000 of contributions they make to a qualified retirement plan—like their Roth IRA. Whether they can claim the credit depends on their income and filing status. To qualify, they must not be a full-time student or be claimed as a dependent on someone else's tax return. They must also be 18 years of age or older and their adjusted gross income must meet certain levels. Check to see if your kid qualifies.

An accountant can help them with the numbers and tax statements, or they can buy a program like Quicken's TurboTax and do it themselves. Just remember that too many people forget to factor in their tax load during the year and are surprised by the large bill they owe on the 15th of April. This often prevents them from taking advantage of additional tax saving techniques such as Health Savings Plans (HSA), charity, 401(k) or IRA plans, and business expenses. Their goal should be to give Uncle Sam the exact amount of money he deserves or that your kid legally owes—and no more.

CREDIT RATING:

The definition of a credit rating is the evaluation or assessment of the creditworthiness of a debtor/borrower. The ratings predict the ability of the borrower to pay back borrowed funds. For individuals, credit ratings are derived from the credit history maintained by credit reporting agencies such as Equifax, Experian, and TransUnion. They typically are used by banks, credit card companies, and credit unions to deem credit worthiness, indicating how much money they will loan you and at what interest rate. The agencies give a credit score or FICO rating of between 300-850, with 850 being the highest score obtainable. FICO comes from the Fair Isaac Corporation, the largest and best known company which provides software for calculating a person's credit score. **Chart 5** shows a Credit Score Rating Chart.

CREDIT SCORE RATINGS CHART

EXCELLENT CREDIT	720-850
GOOD CREDIT	690-719
AVERAGE CREDIT	620-689
BAD CREDIT	300-619

Chart 5

Why is the credit score number important to your kid and why should they check it frequently from some of the free credit reporting sites such as CreditKarma, freecreditreport.com, or Credit Sesame?

First, a good credit rating means they are more likely to get the car, house or college loan they are requesting. Second, and just as important, the better their score, the lower the interest rate a financial institution will charge them. This could mean hundreds or thousands of dollars in interest savings over the course of a car or house loan.

For example, say they take out a $20,000, 60-month car loan and they have poor credit rather than good credit. The difference in credit scores could mean as much as $5,000 more in interest, per the Consumer Federation of America's sixth annual credit score survey.

Or consider the lollapalooza of all debt: a home mortgage. Stacy Johnson from *Money Talk News*, shares this example. “(If you’re) borrowing 200 grand on a 30-year fixed mortgage and show up at the lender’s office with a 620-639 credit score, you’ll pay 4.88 percent. If you make minimum payments, your total interest bill for that mortgage will amount to $181,248 over 30 years. But if you waltz in with a 760 score, you’ll only pay 3.291 percent and your total interest bill over the life of the loan declines to $114,971. That means that over the life of that loan, that lousy score cost you $66,277: Enough to finance your own business, put a kid through a good college, or retire at least a year earlier.”

Finally, a bad credit score could possibly cost your kid the job they really want. Some employers check credit scores to learn whether applicants follow through with their obligations. While interest rates are ever changing and the total dollar amounts differ, the percentage spread for those with excellent credit vs. poor credit is substantial. So yes, good credit is vitally important to your kid’s financial security.

Finally, **Chart 6** shows credit score factors that can negatively affect a credit score. Some of the main ones include:

- Running credit card debts up to the maximum
- Having too many credit cards
- Applying for too many credit cards
- Missing payment due dates on credit cards, your house, student loans, medical expenses, or tax obligations

- Closing unused credit cards could affect your utilization ratio, which accounts for 30% of your credit score

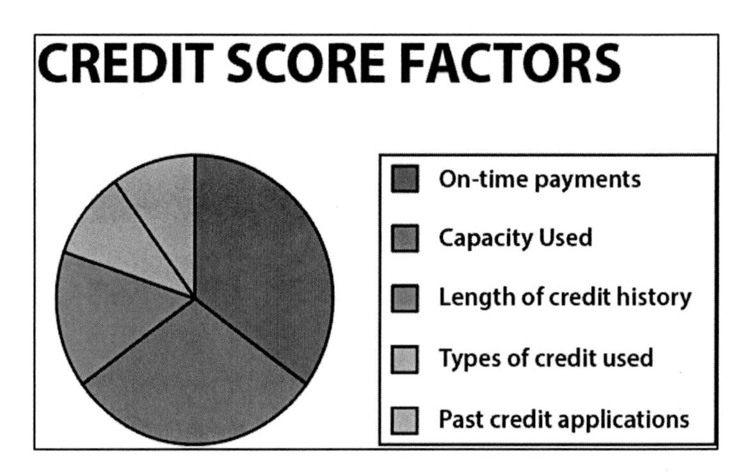

Chart 6

Generally, if they want to keep up a good credit score, they should borrow only if they have income, spend less than they make, pay their bills on time, check their report frequently for discrepancies, and make sure mistakes are disputed. Finally, they should try not to borrow money for things that go down in value—cars, furniture, etc.

ON-LINE APPS / RESOURCES:

While you can put your own personal financial binder together in approximately 10 pages or less per year, there are hundreds of personal BSI packages or investing apps kids can utilize for free or little cost. When they are young, the simpler ones might be best, but this is strictly a personal choice, taking into consideration how they manage their life and commitments. Many financial programs can work, so they should pick the one or two that seem to fit their needs best. One can easily make changes as their BSI needs evolve and as they gain more experience and insight into their finances.

Budgeting app examples:

- Mint
- MoneyPoint
- PowerWallet
- Spending Tracker

Investing Companies or Robo Advisor Programs:

- Betterment: This firm charges 0 .35 percent for accounts between $0 and $10,000 (if you have automatic deposits of $100 or more, $3 a month otherwise); 0.25 percent for accounts between $10,000 and $100,000; and 0.15 percent for accounts holding more than $100,000. There is no minimum deposit or balance and no fees for withdrawals.
- Future Advisor: This firm offers three months of free management but charges a 0.5 percent annual fee. It has no minimum investment requirement.
- LearnVest: LearnVest gives you a financial plan, a real person to talk to, and tools to help make better financial decisions. They charge a one-

time setup fee of $299 plus $19 a month for ongoing support. They are a subsidiary of The Northwestern Mutual Life Insurance Company.

- Personal Capital: Combines sophisticated investing tools with a real live investment advisor. Personal Capital has become known for its free financial software to track your investments. Clients use Personal Capital's software to track their investments, asset allocation, and fees. The cost for its services starts at 0.89% of assets under management.
- WealthFront: A $500 minimum deposit is required. There is no advisory fee for accounts less than $10,000, but this firm charges 0.25 percent on any amount more than $10,000. There is an exchange-traded funds fee of 0.12 percent.
- WiseBanyan: No annual fee and no minimum balance is required. The average expense ratio for its accounts is 0.12 percent.

Note: Robo investing is a very young industry with many entrepreneurial players. Most are funded by venture capitalists and do not make money. There could be significant changes to individual firms regarding their investment style along with frequent mergers and acquisitions in the Robo investing area, so be cautious.

FINANCIAL PLANNING:

Your kids will want to plan for a host of changes in the future. They may change careers, get married, have kids, or simply change as they grow older. At times, we will all need the help of professionals who can guide us through the complexities of wills and trusts, investment assistance, inheritance assistance etc., especially if we are not skilled or eager to learn about these topics. There are numerous companies and financial planning professionals who can be of assistance in your local communities. Find a good one, as they can be a fantastic financial ally for your entire life.

However, have your kids keep learning about their own finances so they can ask the right questions of these individuals, especially regarding fees and costs. Turning their financial life over to someone without paying attention to the expenses involved is very risky, and likely very costly. You don't want them to do this!

COMPOUND INTEREST: RULE OF 72

We have discussed and shared examples of compound interest throughout the book numerous times. It is the tool that allows all kids to become financial secure and must be understood. As we previously noted, Albert Einstein suggested that compound interest is one of man's greatest inventions. He is credited with discovering the mathematical equation—the "Rule of 72."

This rule is a simplified way to determine how long an investment will take to double, given a fixed annual rate of interest. By dividing 72 by the annual rate of return, investors can get a rough estimate of how many years it will take for the initial investment to duplicate itself. The formula for the rule is: Years to double = 72 ÷ interest Rate.

For example, assuming a 10% interest rate, it will take approximately 7 years for your money to double. If you have $10,000 saved by age 20 you will have nearly $1,000,000 saved by age 65, even if you add no additional dollars to your retirement portfolio. However, if you wait till age 30, your $10,000 initial investment will total approximately $320,000 by age 65. That additional 10 years of compounding cost you roughly $600,000. Look at **Table 3**.

Age	Doubled Dollars	Age	Doubled Dollars
20	$10,000	30	$10,000
27	$20,000	37	$20,000
34	$40,000	44	$40,000
41	$80,000	51	$80,000
48	$160,000	58	$160,000
55	$320,000	65	$320,000
62	$640,000		
65	Nearly $1 Million		

Table 3

I am still a believer that a savvy investor can earn the historical average of 10% on your money, but many financial experts suggest 8% is a more appropriate interest rate. So, by using 8%, it would take nine years for your money to double. Throw in some inflation and your overall numbers will be significantly less.

Google.com and KidsVest.org offer several financial calculators you and your kids can utilize to learn and play with your specific numbers.

In summary, the Rule of 72 shows why young people have such a terrific advantage when it comes to wealth generation. Or, as the Rolling Stones sing, "Time, time, time is my side...Yes it is." By educating your kids about the importance of saving and investing early on, "kids can put Einstein's favorite invention to work and gain financial security sooner."

ANGEL INVESTMENT:

If kids understand and apply the budgeting, saving, and investment techniques The Kid$Vest Model affords, then their knowledge, experience, and expertise will typically lead them to investment or entrepreneurial opportunities throughout their life. They can provide terrific ways to increase their wealth, but they do carry more risk. Some opportunities could include buying into a business, starting a company, becoming an angel investor, or simply purchasing stocks or real estate.

In my own career, I bought into a data-based management and direct mail company and started two executive search firms. Many friends of mine invested in non-traditional opportunities at the right moment and have done very well financially. Not having the cash or savings on hand to take advantage of these calculated opportunities means your kid can't play in these wealth enhancement games. But remember, these investments should be funded with discretionary funds that you can afford to lose. As a good friend of mine frequently says, "never bet the farm" on any of these opportunities. Both angel investment and business ownership are discussed below.

As your kids achieve success over their career, they will likely rub shoulders with entrepreneurs who may be creating the next hula hoop craze, pizza chain, or Facebook empire. With solid leadership/management expertise, skills, and/or financial means, they could get involved in these companies as an angel investor. Being an angel investor means lending money to a startup or entrepreneur in the early stages of a company, before it becomes successful and they need huge dollars or go public. How much fun would it be for them to help new entrepreneurs succeed and share in the wealth of their organization's growth?

But remember, both Angel Investing and Business ownership (the next PyraPuzzle piece) are risky at best. They require skill, talent, capital, a long-term horizon, and some luck. A recent article in the Minneapolis Star by long-time business writer Lee Schafer discussed angel investing in his column entitled, *A Word to Wise Angel Investors: It Takes Many At Bats Before You Hit a Home Run.* His article previews successful CEO Darren Cotter, who continues to invest in startup companies and wrote the LinkedIn essay "What I Have Learned in 3 Years of Angel Investing." Mr. Cotter's suggests that:

- You need hands-on experience to become a savvy deal maker—multiple deals

- You should keep one-half of your capital on hand for additional rounds of financing for those companies that show promise
- You must know "the basic math" of angel investing

Cotter's "basic math" suggests that seven of ten investments fail quickly, one of four give you back your initial capital and some return, but only one in twenty might get you a home run—returning at least ten times your investment. These numbers are similar to what other angel investors have shared.

Also, before you think you or your kid knows better or is more skilled at picking the right companies than Mr. Cotter, remember he is a successful CEO/entrepreneur and angel investor. There are numerous horror stories of highly paid professional athletes who have squandered millions of their contract dollars by trying to live richer than they were, or by making lousy investment choices. Mike Tyson, Allen Iverson, Sheryl Swoopes, Dorothy Hamill, Lawrence Taylor, Scottie Pippen, and Michael Vick, are a few famous people who have had money misfortunes.

ENTREPRENEUR / BUSINESS OWNER:

Those who buy into, inherit, or start businesses can have the greatest impact on our society. Business owners create jobs, help grow/build our economy, and personally have a chance at solid wealth building and satisfying careers. Most of American millionaires became rich because they started, or built, an existing business. Liz Weston, a financial writer for *MSN*

Money, said "Create the right business, the upside is all yours. The self-employed not only earn more (their household median income was $75,700 in 2007, compared with $56,600 for employees), but they accumulate dramatically more. The median household net worth of entrepreneurs was $388,700, compared with $93,200 for households whose head worked for somebody else." Remember that starting a business is not a guarantee of financial success.

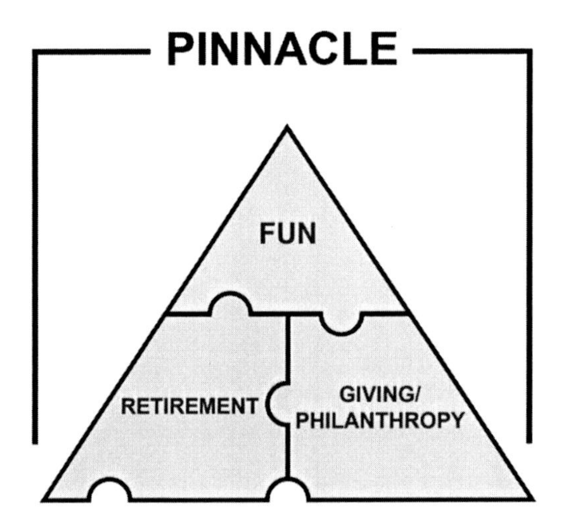

RETIREMENT:

Not everyone wants to retire when they reach 65 years old. Some individuals become successful sooner and leave the workforce early, while some workers need, or want, to work well into their seventies and eighties. Terrific! However, no one wants to work at a job they hate merely for a paycheck, at any age. Following *The Kid$Vest Project* principles will allow your kids to have more choices in their future. They can continue what they are doing, give back philanthropically, or spend more time on their favorite hobby. They have earned the right to pursue any of these options during their retirement years, since they wisely spent their life applying the DreamLife principles.

GIVING / PHILANTHROPY:

There are terrific examples of successful people who are now giving back to society with dollars that are impacting millions of lives. Bill and Melinda Gates, Warren Buffet, and Mark and Priscilla Zuckerberg immediately come to mind as individuals who are shaping the future of healthcare and education. But there are people all over the country who are giving substantial sums of money to terrific causes or educational systems to foster learning, ease suffering, and provide affordable housing (Habitat for Humanity).

Just because your kids can't offer income to organizations they support doesn't mean they can't contribute. There are millions of Americans who are offering their most precious resource—their time. I personally was involved with The Raptor Center at the University of Minnesota for seven years, serving four of them as the Board Chair. I currently serve as the Chair of the Supervisory Committee for a large credit union. Both opportunities have been great experiences for me. I have received much more than I've given while serving these quality organizations. Each kid should find their own niche and passion for continued growth and giving back.

FUN: Living A Life You Love

As I've said before, if your kids are not enjoying their life's journey, what is the point? Remember, while they are amassing wealth, paying down bills, and/or successfully investing throughout their life, make sure your kids "smell the roses along the way." Giving back and having fun must be incorporated throughout their life for their own personal DreamLife to be meaningful.

As parents, it is our duty to make Fun an important part of our children's lives.

In conclusion, learning and mastering the Dream-Life PyraPuzzle skills in their youth, and throughout their careers, will ultimately lead your kids to financial success. There are specific books and on-line articles printed daily about the various sections of the PyraPuzzle. Have your kids refer to them or visit the KidsVest.org website for more detailed information. When we can interest more states and school systems in advancing the DreamLife principles in our K-12 grades, America will be on its way to decreasing our wealth gap and growing a vibrant middle-class!

"All our dreams can come true—if we have the courage to pursue them."

Walt Disney

Chapter FIVE

LIFE'S BIG FINANCIAL MOMENTS

If your kids are already applying *The Kid$Vest Project principles,* they are well on their way to financial prosperity. Good for them! It means you have taught and had them practice budgeting, saving, and investing techniques. It also means that they have showed patience and spending restraint (delayed gratification) in their daily life. They haven't let seemingly innocent small bills add up to a blown budget.

These are all admirable qualities that can lead them to their own personal DreamLife. This strategically designed lifestyle may never make them "stupid wealthy," but most of their needs and some of their wants will likely be obtainable. That would make any Kid$Vest member proud of them. It should be great waking up in the morning, looking in the mirror and knowing that they can pursue a career or hobby that satisfies them.

Being conscientious about the small budget leaks that can drain their financial system is important. Try to help your kids review and reduce their daily or monthly expenses such as internet, phone and living expenses, etc. For example, Stacy Johnson's article in *MoneyTalksNews* uses data from the placement firm, Accounting Life. He notes that "50% of American workers regularly buy coffee at work to the tune of $1,000 per year and 66% buy lunch at an average of $37 dollar per week, or $2,000 per year. That total $3,000 for coffee and lunch totals $90,000 in 30 years ($3,000 x 30 years). From our compounding knowledge, that translates into $200,000 ($250 per month x 30 years @ 5%) you could have had in your savings or retirement account." Small savings add up over time and can greatly enhance an investment portfolio.

This chapter will highlight the major expenses that could also make or break your kid's DreamLife and help or hinder them from reaching their ultimate financial goals. These big items are going to come along in their life sooner than they think, so they might as well understand and prepare for them.

What are the most frequent *Big Ticket* items that could positively or negatively impact young lives in the future? Here are five of the most important.

1. Cars
2. College—Undergraduate and Graduate Degrees
3. Houses
4. Marriage
5. Family—kids

Your kids can budget, save, and invest well, set up an emergency fund, and protect their assets with insurance as needed, but all can be for naught if they mess up major purchases over their lifetime. These items often require large dollar outlays over long periods of time. For example, say they splurge and compromise their budget on a spring vacation to Fort Lauderdale, which they put on their credit card. Unless this trip is paid for by you, they've just blown a month or three of their budget. However, all of us make trips, buy that favorite new coat, or have a Café Vanilla Frappuccino coffee from time to time. We should have some fun along life's journey, right? Without a little splurging along the way, what is the point?

Spending on cars, college, house, marriage, and family are big deals that can bankrupt all their positive efforts for years instead of months and add more financial stress to their life. Financial stress will be further discussed in Chapter 8, The Health & Wealth Killers. For now, let's take a closer look at each one of these large capital outlays for some insight about their impact on your kid's financial life.

CARS: Depreciating Assets

Somewhere between the ages of 16 and 20 they will probably own their first car, and for some very good reasons. They may need one to get to school, extracurricular activities, or work. If they are not lucky enough to be able to use one of the family cars, or are given one outright, they should be very careful about initiating this large cash outlay. I was always jealous of a friend of mine who was given a brand-new Cutlass Supreme for graduation, while I had to purchase a 10-year-old Plymouth Valiant that cost me $117 per month for three years. After all, he started out $1,400 richer than me per year. He didn't have to pay for his car. If I wouldn't have been making car payments, I could have put $5,200 dollars more in my Roth IRA over those three years—over $400,000 in 40 years. Where was Kid$Vest when I was growing up? However, my Valiant did have one feature my friend's Cutlass couldn't match. That was my Moo Cow horn. When pushed on numerous country roads where cattle were grazing, the herd often came running. True story, but I still think my friend came out better financially!

Also, as kids budget for their new set of wheels, remember that the additional expenses of owning and operating a vehicle are not cheap. Service, gas/oil, insurance, taxes, license plate tabs, and parking will add significantly to their monthly expenses. College parking alone could cost them $1,000 annually. So, if they have some flexibility like biking, walking, or using city mass transit, try to persuade them to utilize these methods first. They can save big by not purchasing a car until they go to college or waiting until they graduate.

I know this is a hard pill to swallow when friends and relatives have cars of their own, but that $5,000-10,000 loan could turn out to be a game-changer in their Roth IRA. "Looking like you are worth a lot is not really being worth a lot," as Stacy Johnson says. If Kid$Vest teaches your kids nothing else, remember instant gratification can be harmful to their investment future. Instead of owning a depreciating asset such as a car, especially an expensive car, they can deposit the money in their saving, investment, or Roth IRA accounts and make themselves $500,000 to $750,000 when they turn 60/65. As I said before, delayed gratification is a bummer.

My advice to any young person who didn't just win the lottery, NEVER BUY A NEW CAR. Or at least make sure if they do buy new, they get the deal of the century. Once their budget dictates what price point they can afford, there are plenty of dealers selling leased cars that are 2-3 years old and have been driven fewer than 30,000 miles (almost a new car in today's world) for $5-15,000 less than a new car. Or they can be really "cool" and buy that safe, good runner that might look pretty beat up. Why purchase a new car that loses 10% of its value as soon as they drive it off the lot?

Know and share with them that most millionaires they pass on the street are typically unrecognizable in their Buicks, Chevys and Hyundais. They simply don't want the attention the Porsche, Lamborghini, and Ferrari drivers receive at your local country clubs. Truth be told, there are many more millionaires living in modest neighborhoods than in some of the more upscale communities near you. Why? Because these frugal residents are spending less and saving more for their retirement, rather than living paycheck to paycheck as so called more affluent residents often do. A report on economic well-being of U.S. households noted that 57% of Americans are living paycheck to paycheck.

Your kids will likely own 10-25 vehicles over the course of their lifetime. Paying attention to year-end sales, price negotiation, discontinued models, forgoing high priced options and finding low cost financing (perhaps at your credit union) can save them a staggering amount of money over their lifetime.

The absolute best auto deal in my lifetime was the purchase of a 2004 Ranger pickup truck. It was the end of the year in 2004, which is the best time of the year for car deals. I searched every Ford dealership in the Twin Cities for the best deal. Forty minutes from home on the other side of town, I talked to a salesman who said he had the best deal. I viewed the truck, and we negotiated a price of $14,000 on this brand-new vehicle. The sticker price was approximately $22,000 (their discount was originally at $16,500). I left and went to another dealership, but found the previous dealer's price was the best I could do. So when the salesman called me back, I agreed to buy the truck and said I would come into the dealership later that day.

That afternoon I showed up and the salesman looked at me and said, "We just sold the truck you were looking at." Being a good guy, he also said "we can't have an unhappy customer, so he made me this counter-offer. For $14,750 dollars, I could have the same vehicle with power windows and doors, a six CD changer and the towing package. Done deal—I bought the truck.

How do I know it was a great deal? Well, being a salesman myself, I asked the finance VP how they could sell me this truck at that low price. He responded by saying that Ford was in a battle with Chevy over truck sales and they had a money pool they could access. Then, for some unknown reason, I stopped at one final dealership just to make sure my deal was the best one. I know, overkill! This new salesman pulled up the computer listing of all new Ranger trucks in the Twin Cities and said I couldn't buy that truck at that price anywhere. When I showed him my sales slip, he shook his head and said I got a great deal. That's when I knew I had the best deal I could get!

The rest of the story, as Paul Harvey would say, was that I drove this truck until I sold it in 2015 for $9,000. It obviously kept its value and it had low miles on it, but that truck cost me only $5,705 dollars over the 11 years I owned it. That works out to $523 dollars per year, plus gas, maintenance and insurance. I am still proud of this deal!

To be sure, I was very lucky on this car negotiation. But before making offers and wandering into the dealership like a lamb to the slaughter, I knew the following:

- The true value of the vehicle—not just the monthly payment
- I knew what my budget was and stuck to it

- I bought the highest quality, low-mileage, well-maintained vehicle I could afford
- I found a motivated dealership or private party willing to deal
- I was willing to walk away from several deals until I found the best one

COLLEGE: A Huge Expense, But an Appreciating Asset

It is still extremely beneficial for kids to attend college, at least from a financial standpoint. Getting a degree can significantly increase their chances of earning more income and positional power in their career. In Chapter Three, The DreamLife PyraPuzzle, we showed the disparity of income and net worth between individuals with GEDs, college undergraduate and graduate school degrees. Also, the experience, socialization, and future contacts made during this four-year period can be important.

How they go about getting their degree and/or paying for it, varies widely by kid and family, income, and career. That is, your kid can pay and work as they go, accept student loans, or receive scholarships to help defer educational costs. If you can afford and offer to pay for your kids' education, don't have them immediately apply to the most expensive schools. Depending on the college or university they wish to attend, it could cost you approximately $15,000-$65,000 a year for the next four years ($60,000 to $260,000). This kind of cash outflow, whether through loans or cash, could be severely detrimental to your own personal financial lives.

Have discussions with your kids about their empathy for your financial health, if only because they might have to take care of you down the road. And they should realize the expense of having you pay for their brother or sister's college as well. If you don't already have one to five million dollars set aside for retirement, you might be mortgaging your future. Parents and kids should have these frank discussions before colleges are considered or discussed.

If you recall the chapter on career goals, knowing themselves is very important at this point. Understanding their strengths, passions, and career goals is the first step in their educational journey beyond high school. You should help them be smart about their college decisions. And also remember the gap year strategy. A new book out by Jeff Selingo titled *There is Life After College* may be worth a read as well. Selingo says "College is generally worth the price, but only if your kids graduate. If not, they will become one of the 50 million Americans who don't have the piece of paper, but likely have college debt." Make certain they have the determination to finish, otherwise they'll be worse off financially than if they hadn't gone to college in the first place.

If your kids are thinking about potential colleges, here are some questions to discuss:

- Who will be paying for the college costs
- What career paths might be possible
- What types of schools are available to them (via grades and SAT scores)

- What type of loans and how many will be needed over the four-year (or longer) college timeline
- What kind of scholarships are possible
- What is the true cost of college and loans, and what kind of payments will they need to make once they graduate—DO THE MATH together

If you aren't paying for your kid's education, then all the above costs will defer to them. Without proper planning, they could be making the same devastating financial mistakes mentioned previously.

Options, please! If you are well-off and decide to pay for your kid's educations, they can likely go any place they desire. They should go, learn a lot, and have fun—but they should come away with their degree in four years. It won't guarantee a great job or a successful career, but it is a good entry ticket or starting point for their career.

If you are going to pay, but have limited resources, help your kids pick schools that fit well within their potential vocation or career aspirations and budget. For example, going to Harvard to become an elementary education teacher is certainly overkill. Or if they don't have specific career aspirations yet, then getting a degree from a less pricey college or university offers them alternatives. There is no harm in going to a trade school or junior college to learn more about their strengths and career desires. They can always transfer to a 4-year school for the remaining two years. Or they can take college courses in high school, as many students successfully do. Just make sure that the college classes they take in high school or at a junior college will transfer to the college they later attend. Early planning is the key!

Finally, there is no law that says they must earn their degree in four years, right out of high school. They can take a few classes and work along the way, as their financial status requires. They are most likely going to work for more than 40 years, so starting towards their goals more slowly and deliberately may save them a lot of financial pain.

If they have learned and practiced the Kid$Vest techniques and saved $4,000-10,000 dollars in a Roth IRA before they attend college, they will still be well on their way to financial security. They can easily catch up to or pass their peers who went to college right away without this strategy and have large school loans after graduation. There is no disgrace in having them earn a degree later in their life. The timing of their education is up to both of you, and often dependent on your financial situation. However, stretching a four-year degree out over five or six years because they aren't motivated or can't decide on a major is wasteful. And it is very expensive, if you are footing the bill. So make sure your kids are respectful of your time and money.

Additional items to pay attention to include: in-state versus out-of-state tuition, proximity to home versus housing costs, part-time work, grade transfer ability, student loan packages, etc. These should be factored into college discussions with your kids because over 50% of college graduates have $41,000 in student loan debt and $4,000 in credit card debt. This expenditure can be worth it, but it should be well thoughtout in advance.

In summary, perhaps the encouraging story of Katie will inspire you. She is a single, 31-year-old woman who in 2015 completely paid off her school debt. Katie grew up the daughter of hard-working, blue collar parents in the Twin Cities, typical of working class households in America. However, Katie's parents instilled in her that success comes from education, employment, and at times, practicing delayed gratification. She was a lifeguard during the summers before college and since she was smart, earned a scholarship from a local business.

She graduated from the University of Minnesota in 2007 with a B.S. in Biology and a minor in Chemistry. Even with her partial scholarship, Katie still had amassed $41,000 in school debt. But here is where Katie differs from most young adults today. Her parents taught her the value of always living within her means. She also took advantage of high school AP classes to limit college expenses. This industrious young woman not only turned an internship into her first full-time job, she worked weekends at a local airline to pay down her student loans. She continued to live at home and drive a paid-off used car. In 2015, she made her last school loan payment. With no debt and a solid job, Katie finally purchased a new car as a way of celebrating. And the best news, due to her parent's encouragement Katie also contributed to her IRA and 401(k) the entire time, using a classic *pay yourself first mentality*.

So Katie got her degree, paid off her debt, and took advantage of compound interest to the tune of saving $45,000, all by the time she was 31 years old. While she admitted that her early personal life maybe wasn't as exciting as some of her peers, it was relatively stress-free. She had a plan she was executing toward a successful life. She was also able to do some travelling. Better yet, Katie's future now looks very promising, doesn't it? This is a classic story of what *The Kid$Vest Project* wants to instill in all American kids. I couldn't be any prouder of her life style choices—congratulations Katie!

HOUSE(S): Big Expense, But Potentially Terrific Appreciating Asset

My wife and I have made substantial money on our houses over the years. For example, our first house was a townhouse near Washington D.C. We bought it for $52,000 and sold it for $72,000 18 months later—a whopping 40% return! Then we purchased a home in Dellwood, Minnesota, where we lived and raised our family for 21 years. The large lot was spectacular, but the house was an older rambler. Ten years before we sold it we made significant improvements (when we could afford to). When we did sell, it was for a significantly higher price. And this didn't include the real estate tax deductions. We were both lucky and astute on these transactions!

We bought houses that were slight budget stretches, but they had some nice amenities in the best location we could afford. In the case of the last example, the house barely appreciated for 15 of the 21 years we lived in it. However, in the last 5 years, the market was on fire and we earned an excellent return on our money.

Here is what I've learned about making money in real estate:

- Don't buy a house just to buy a house. Make sure it fits into your budget and is a good financial deal. Especially when you are young, you want flexibility for jobs and relocation.
- At the right time, buy a nice property or house in the best area you can afford. Location! Location! Location!
- Try to make a deal when the real estate market is down, and sell when it is rising. This means you may not be buying or selling at *your* most optimum time personally, but at the *market's* optimum time. You must have patience and keep an eye on the real estate market to make this strategy work. This is especially true if you are talking about rental property you may own in the future.
- In general, if you must sell your home due to loss of a job, relocation, divorce, or poor market timing, it is likely you will either lose money or not get as much as you could. Sometimes you have no choice, but if you do, you will always come out ahead.
- The better negotiation skills you have, the more money you will save or earn. We sold this last house with a realtor on a 60-day contract at a reduced fee. We knew our house was very sellable in a *hot* market. It sold in 30 days! That little negotiation saved us 3%.

- If you have creative or physical talent in upgrading or remodeling, and you do the work yourself, or you realize your limitations and hire an interesting designer to make your property more appealing, you generally will do better financially over the long term.
- Never buy the largest or most expensive house in the neighborhood. Your upside potential will be limited, no matter what transpires in the years to come.
- If you want the best deal, try not to fall in love with your home before you buy it—it is after all, an investment.

You can't always choose the timing to make the best financial deal when you're buying and selling real estate. If you can, your investment return will generally be higher. Some people think of real estate as housing and some think of it as their home or castle. I think of it as both! We had fun raising our kids in a great home for 21 years, but when the market caught fire and the kids were grown, we downsized our house and made some extra money. Then we moved to a new home to start the process over. This time we got caught in the market crash of 2008, so we are patiently waiting for the market to turn around before we sell our existing residence and buy a place in a warmer climate. Rinse and repeat!

Also, over the years we have taken advantage of low interest rates and refinancing options because the economy the last ten years allowed us to benefit by doing so. It made financial sense. For example, we refinanced during a downswing in interest rates and saved $300 a month on our mortgage payment. We knew we would be in the house for at least the next five years, so the reduced payment allowed us to cover the closing cost in less than a year. This was a smart thing to do in our situation. Additionally, we took advantage of the IRS rules of selling our house and not having to pay taxes on gains (up to $500,000 per couple). "To claim the whole exclusion, you must have owned and lived in your home as your principal residence an aggregate of at least two of the five years before the sale (this is called the ownership and use test). You can claim this exclusion once every two years."

Everyone might not be as lucky with interest rates or house appreciation in the next 10-20 years, so it's important to make decisions based on changing economic situations. For example, some of the nice profits we made on houses may be tough to repeat with baby boomers reducing the size of their houses and rising interest rates.

My bottom line on housing is that once your kids have a stable job reasonably close to where they live, they can start putting in some offers. This is especially true if rents in their area are comparable to buying. Remember to teach them the negotiation techniques we previously discussed and most importantly, what type of house and expenses their budget allows. Try to suggest that they "fit into their mortgage" over the next few years and then improve their property so the value rises. Then as their income hopefully increases over time, they will have a few dollars to reinvest in their home.

Have them redo their kitchen, master bedroom, great room or bathrooms, rather than adding a pool. The pool will be discounted, at least in Minnesota, by most buyers when it's time to sell the property. If they are astute, are patient, and hit the market at the right time, they should be able to gain net-worth appreciation with home ownership. Their home can still be their castle!

MARRIAGE: Potentially Awesome Appreciating Asset

Thank goodness most American kids who choose the marriage route are waiting longer. I'm certainly not against marriage, especially when they find the one they want to spend their life with. Warren Buffett always says that one of the best investments he ever made was to pick a great life partner. However, really knowing your future spouse when you are both more financially and emotionally mature, is a good thing. Take it from someone who has been married for more than forty years to the same woman!

People who are a bit older seem to know themselves, their passions, their career aspirations, and family desires better. Discussions about money and lifestyle can be more fruitful and take on new meaning to more mature young adults. My advice to any young adults is to completely understand their future spouse's income and spending habits, current debts, and credit rating so you both know what you are taking on together. You might think this takes love out of the equation or that my comments are cold and calculating. Well, talk to friends and relatives who have been "halved and quartered" (married two or three times) and see how well off they are financially.

Nancy Dunham in a *MoneyTalksNews* article notes, "It is easy to forget that marriage is more than joining two lives and families. It's also a business contract. That business contract can benefit you financially, but there are ways that it can also torpedo your finances now and in the future." A survey by SunTrust found 35% of married couples cited money as the number one stress in marriage.

On the positive side, Liz Weston used some census data in a recent article (Census Bureau wealth study) to show that the median net worth of married couple households was more than four to five times higher than single men or women. "Furthermore, married couples' wealth increased at the faster pace of 16% a year, compared with 8% for single people. That suggests that couples who stay together will build substantially more wealth over their lifetimes than two comparable singles." So best of luck to your kids in finding a life partner who lights up their life and their finances—a winning combination for a happy life!

And here is some advice about your kid's wedding day! There is no reason to overspend on his/her wedding by throwing a one-day bash that decimates your/their saving strategy for years to come. Kid$Vest graduates are smarter than that! This is true even if you can afford to be more generous. Their wedding should be thoughtfully planned and expensed so no hardships are created for you or them. In fact, their wedding can be a great opportunity to get a jump on their financial well-being. For example, if you have a budget for your kids to spend, anything under that budget could go into their pockets. They get the difference! This can be used for future savings, investments, or perhaps help fund their Roth IRA plan. Now we're talking!

As an example, I went to a business associate's wedding some years ago, where the young couple received approximately $20,000 from friends and family. They hoped their kids would put the money towards their first business. I think this idea has some teeth in it. What if kids asked guests for a contribution to their Roth IRA to get the newlyweds off on the proper financial foot? Sounds cold now, but wait a few years and they'll be thrilled with the financial outcome! When I was the President of the James J. Hill Center, we did 50-70 weddings annually. I saw many couples or families who could have benefited from a more conservative wedding day celebration.

FAMILY & KIDS: Expensive Depreciating Asset, But The Most Rewarding One of Your Life.

I would not even begin to touch the subject of when and how many children your kids should have. This is not China! Many couples love kids and want a bunch of them—God bless them.

I would only offer these comments to parents that they can share with their kids:

- Each child will cost them approximately $245,000 to raise to age eighteen. So they should plan how they will pay for their kids. One year of college tuition for average college expenses will cost them an additional $24,061 to $47,831 per year, depending on in-state versus out-of-state tuition and public versus private school costs.

- It is your duty to teach your kids financial literacy knowledge and action steps early in their lives so they can later obtain their own personal DreamLife.

Having said this, parenthood has been the most gratifying and fun experience my wife and I have ever had.

In summary, to achieve financial happiness, we must pay attention to both the large and small purchases during our life. Application of the strategic knowledge and actions plans *The Kid$Vest Project* teaches should put your kids on a DreamLife path. Good luck to them and may they have a boatload of fun along the way!

"It is my land (life). Who would I be if I did not try to make it better."

Orlando Bloom, Kingdom of Heaven

Chapter SIX

JUST FOR FUN, HOW TO BECOME A MILLIONAIRE!

The Kid$Vest Project of financial education and action steps will take some significant planning and a bundle of patience for most American kids and their parents. Perhaps a little faith as well! So just for some fun, let's look at some potential ways they can make their first million dollars. Remember, FUN must be part of their everyday life to obtain a true DreamLife.

Your kids can win or earn their first million by:

- Hitting the PowerBall Jackpot—spending their excess cash buying lotto tickets for the slim chance of being that one in four hundred million that wins

- Inheriting wealth—you pass on your good fortune to them
- Having a successful career
- Starting or buying a business—successful entrepreneurs or business owners are often among the wealthiest group in our society
- Employing *The Kid$Vest Project Principles*, if none of the above seem likely to be in the cards for them.

Sure, there are numerous ways that we can become millionaires. But for most of us, we must be frugal with our money and diligently save and invest to reach this milestone. In Chapter four, The DreamLife Pyra-Puzzle, we discussed career growth and how many Americans have used their talent, expertise, and luck to have successful careers. Assuming they practice BSI techniques, their lives can be financially secure with limited financial stress.

Another way to become a millionaire, is to take your creativity and become a business owner or entrepreneur. We know that innovation and entrepreneurship continue to drive most countries economically, including the United States. Creating environments where these opportunities can thrive has become a community and governmental priority. This is one reason why business obstacles like excessive federal regulation and lack of capital are such political "hot buttons" nationally and at the state level.

We do see some terrific *green shoots* of entrepreneur education, development, and implementation in cities across our country. Cities on the forefront of assisting and pushing entrepreneurialism include Boulder and Denver, Colorado, Fargo, North Dakota, Kansas City, Missouri, and Austin, Texas. These are in addition to historically entrepreneurial cities like Silicon Valley, Boston, the Triangle in North Carolina, and New York City.

I learned about and helped develop some of these models when I was the President of the James J. Hill Center in downtown St. Paul, MN. This reference library offered resources for gathering business data and sharing entrepreneurial stories in the Twin Cities. Our mission at The Hill was "connecting entrepreneurs, business and community." Assisting small business and startups are important because we know that future job growth depends on this kind of economic development.

Other positive traits these communities have in common include: strong universities, innovative and large corporate organizations and foundations, legislature and political support, and visionary entrepreneurial leaders who are making it easier for businesses to grow. America is trying to maintain its entrepreneur culture, although the growth of startups is not nearly as fast as we need for a larger economy.

But let's remember a couple of things about the reality of entrepreneurship. Starting a business is certainly no guarantee it will succeed. Per Bloomberg, eight out of ten entrepreneurs fail within the first 18 months. The Small Business Administration data is less harsh and suggests that when a small business employs at least one person besides the owner, 70% survive at least two years, 50% make it for five years, and 25% last up to 15 years. Regardless of whose numbers you want to believe, starting or building a business is not for the faint of heart.

Successful entrepreneurs are people with terrific vision, problem solving skills, a host of leadership traits, and a little luck. If your kids have the idea, the persistence, and some financially backing, encourage them to go for it! Entrepreneurship can be a very satisfying and financially rewarding career move. Just make sure they have a well thought out backup plan or exit timeline, in case things don't work out.

Let's also talk about $1,000,000 as a financial milestone. First, it is a lot of money, especially if kids are just starting out with minimum dollars in their retirement account or they are working for minimum wage. At 15-20 years old, it likely seems a very distant goal. Second, one million dollars is still a benchmark, and a solid first goal along the way to a desirable retirement nest-egg. Under the typical retirement scenario of taking 4% of principal to live on, 4% of $1,000,000 is $40,000 per year. After taxes and healthcare in retirement, there might not much left. Your Millennial kids who rationalize that they don't care if they ever become a millionaire, realize that they will care someday.

Before you get all stressed out or discouraged that your kids will never have a chance to achieve financial security, think about the life of Ronald Read. He recently passed away in Vermont at the age of 92. This gas station attendant and janitor was a multi-millionaire and was touted in the press for leaving five million dollars to his local hospital and library. Mr.

Read was known for his modest lifestyle, but he obviously was good at BSI. There are thousands of people like Mr. Read in communities across America. By practicing the Kid$Vest techniques, your kids can still reach financial freedom.

And before we show a few more strategies that can add to a youth's wealth nest egg, let's take one last look at the compound interest concept. Why? Because true understanding of this concept is vital to the success of *The Kid$Vest Project* and youth wealth. Remember the old game of "Would You Rather." *Would you rather have—option 1: A gift of one million dollars or Option 2: one penny doubled each day for 30 days? Most of you know this example, but....*

Day 1: *$.01*
Day 2: *$.02*
Day 3: $.04
Day 4: $.08
Day 5: $.16
Day 6: $.32
Day 7: $.64
Day 8: $1.28
Day 9: $2.56
Day 10: $5.12
Day 11: $10.24
Day 12: $20.48
Day 13: $40.96
Day 14: $81.92
Day 15: $163.84
Day 16: $327.68
Day 17: $655.36

Day 18: $1,310.72
Day 19: $2,621.44
Day 20: $5,242.88
Day 21: $10,485.76
Day 22: $20,971.52
Day 23: $41,943.04
Day 24: $83,886.08
Day 25: $167,772.16
Day 26: $335,544.32
Day 27: $671,088.64
Day 28: $1,342,177.28
Day 29: $2,684,354.56
Day 30: $5,368,709.1215

Obviously, you would rather have option B—a penny doubled each day for 30 days. While this is not true compounding (earning interest on principal and interest), this example is another way of showing why we want your kids to fund their personal Roth IRA when they are as young as possible. The extra five to seven years in their teens or early twenties makes a big difference in their total retirement dollars saved over their 40-year career.

Notice the last seven days in the example above, dollars generated go from approximately $83,000 to over $5,000,000. The big leaps in the amount occur during the last few days, don't they? Similar large increases can occur in your kid's Roth IRA or 401(k) portfolios as they get closer to retirement. By starting to save and invest sooner, the dollar amounts rise dramatically, just when they're young enough to enjoy them. That is, the money builds quickly toward the end of their 40-year career, just in time for them to sail off into their retirement sunset. That is, if retirement is their goal!

No one has ever come up to me and suggested they would double my money for a month and I suspect no one has recently knocked on your door either. We've got to find another way for our kids to become financially secure. Kid$Vest's philosophy of investing a small amount of capital while they are young, then letting this capital simmer over time (about 40 years) will also get them there.

Bill Cooper, former CEO and Chairman of TCF bank, was often asked why his bank so enthusiastically marketed free checking accounts to his customers. You see, checking accounts are typically low or small profit accounts. Bill would laugh and say, "A small number times a big number is still a big number." He was referring to bank profits. So, have your kids put as much as they can in their Roth IRA before their 20th birthday, have them sprinkle in some additional dollars in their company 401(k) during their career and then have them wait for 40-45 years. Voila! They should have well over $1,000,000 by the time they're in their sixties, and most of it will be tax advantaged in retirement!

This is certainly a vast improvement over the current average American's retirement savings of $50,000. Let alone the 56% of Americans who have saved less than $10,000 for retirement. Finally, if you consider that the Bureau of Labor Statistics says Americans 65 years or older average $44,686 in annual expenses, we are collectively in sad financial shape.

This is an American tragedy! *The Kid$Vest Project* can make all the difference.

OTHER WAYS TO MAKE LIFE FINANCIALLY EASIER

To take advantage of the *miracle of compounding*, there are alternative ways our government, parents, and grandparents can help kids reach their first million-dollar milestone. Some of them include:

- 529 plans
- Gifting—parents and grandparents
- KidSave and ASPIRE Act

529 Plans:

If you are a parent or grandparent, you can set up a 529 Plan for your kids or grandkids at birth or any time thereafter. The 529 college-savings plans were created in 1997 by the Internal Revenue Code Section 529, which allows individuals to grow college savings in tax-free programs sponsored by the states. Study your state's plans to make sure they fit your family's interests and goals since there are positives and negatives to consider. You can get advice and help from your CPA, a financial advisor, or the Internal Revenue Service (IRS) website. Michelle Perry Higgins, financial planner and principal at California Financial Advisors, shares some of the advantages of the 529 plan:

- The earnings that accumulate are tax-deferred, withdrawals are exempt from federal income tax and are also generally exempt from state tax for "qualified higher education expenses" (books, supplies, tuition, fees, room and board). Note: This does NOT include a new car or a shopping spree for the beneficiary.

- The beneficiary and account holder must be identified when opening the account. After that, friends and family members can also contribute to the plan.
- If the beneficiary does not use all the funds or decides not to attend college, the account holder can change the beneficiary to another family member (i.e. sibling, parent).
- Funds may be used at any eligible higher education institution in the U.S. as well as some colleges overseas.
- The minimum contribution is typically very low, thus making it more affordable for families to get started. Also, the maximum contribution is quite high, often around $250,000.
- The account holder has control of the funds, not the beneficiary.

Some of the disadvantages of the 529 plan are:

- Plans will vary from state to state, which make it a little more challenging for families. You need to do your due diligence on the sales charges, fees, and investment choices by the plan administrator.
- When a withdrawal is made, but not used for "qualified higher education expenses," the

earnings may be subject to income tax plus a 10% penalty tax.
- A 529 account may reduce your beneficiary's ability to receive financial aid.

My personal experience with 529 Plans comes from the four I set up for my granddaughters. There is nothing complicated about doing them, my only caution is that you take enough risk in the funds you choose, especially when your child or grandchild is young. You can become more conservative in investment choices as the kids get closer to college age.

Gifting:

The IRS also allows for parents and grandparents to gift $14,000 a year from each spouse and/or grandparent (a total of $56,000) to certain relatives, including their kids. Obviously, this allows wealthier families to transfer income to family members without being taxed. This funneling of money to family members is a great way to share dollars that can benefit family members during one's lifetime. However, as mentioned above, this precludes most families with modest or low incomes.

KidSave & ASPIRE Act:

Two additional potential saving programs include The KidSave and ASPIRE Act. The KidSave plan is being touted by former Senator Bob Kerry from Nebraska. He and others have been suggesting that every child born in the United States would receive $1,000 in a KidSave account that would compound over 65 years before being tapped. As Kerry noted in an article by Dan Kadlec, “For most people it's not income that matters...it's wealth accumulation.” The total dollars at 6% over 65 years would accrue approximately $44,145 in tax-deferred savings.

Maybe not a huge pile to draw on, but Kerry goes on to say that “the existence of a wealth account from birth would encourage more savings.” While various options of this plan could earn even more dollars, it sounds like a fair and simple program that would give all American kids a chance to put some money away at birth. This program was initially discussed in the 1990's and has still not been implemented.

In 2006, an idea was recommended to simply give $500 to each child at birth and allow it to grow tax free until age 65. The so-called ASPIRE Act would also allow kids to continue adding to their account over time. The purpose of the accounts, says Reid Cramer, the director of the Asset Building Program at the New America Foundation, would be to get people invested in their futures. “Having an asset has the potential to change the way people think and plan for their future, and sometimes those effects can be generated just from small asset holdings.” He goes on to say, “It's possible for people to build significant savings over time.” The ASPIRE Act also would pair the creation of the accounts with financial literacy programs in schools.

Pioneering research by University of Michigan professor Michael Sherraden suggests starting savings accounts for lower-income people can lead them to feel more confident about the future. Recipients of such accounts also report feeling that they have greater control over their lives, including the ability to plan for education and retirement costs.

Do any of the last few paragraphs sound familiar to you—perhaps like the Kid$Vest education and action steps? I certainly hope so! Unfortunately, these plans have never seen the light of day! Kadlec asks "Why dust off KidSave now? Because it is a relatively painless way to address retirement shortfalls in the future. But as the youngest boomers and Gen Xers retire with virtually no guaranteed income other than Social Security, the shortfall will only grow." This shortfall Kadlec is talking about is the lack of retirement dollars Americans have in their retirement portfolios—which leads to the wealth gap we discussed. Politicians and American citizens alike need to ask themselves why these worthwhile programs have not been implemented. Of course, *The Kid$Vest Project* is not waiting for government assistance or an answer.

Imagine if the KidSave program was initiated at the same time parents begin funding their newborns 529 Plan and a Roth IRA was funded by your kids before they reached 20 years old. Finally, financially knowledgeable kids would become adults who have budgeted, saved, and invested in IRA and 401(k) plans throughout their lives. Assuming average investment returns, this is as close to a sure thing as you can get.

The one million dollars we discussed in this chapter would only be a milestone, not the result. No, their final number would be significantly higher! It is time to make *The Kid$Vest Project* and other financial literacy programs a part of our American culture—for the sake of our kids and to create a stronger, more vibrant middle class.

"To accomplish great things, we must not only act, but also dream; not only plan, but also believe."

Anatole France

Chapter SEVEN

THE HEALTH AND WEALTH KILLERS—STRESS & DEBT

I have always believed in the development of the total person—mind and body. I learned from my father's example that one without the other simply does not create the balance needed to obtain a true DreamLife. The Kid$Vest mission is "Building youth wealth through financial education and investment action." If you and your kids subscribe to its principles throughout life, they should have the financial freedom to live a life they'll love.

However, if they don't get enough sleep, exercise moderately, or eat a healthy diet, they may not have the physical stamina to enjoy the fruits of their labor. That would be a tragedy. Of course, the most important health advice we can offer our kids is:

Don't smoke, or if they do, help them quit!

Too many of us take our health for granted, especially when we are young. We think we are bullet-proof or immune to sickness and accidents! We all have friends or relatives that daily prove us wrong in these beliefs, but we have a hard time fathoming that these misfortunes could happen to us too.

For someone who still enjoys athletics and fitness, staying in good physical shape has been relatively easy. I like exercising! This is not the case for everyone; we all have our gifts, likes, and dislikes. Early in my father's career as a coach and teacher, he taught physical education. His goal was not to make super stars, or even athletes, out of his students. His only real goal was to teach his students that everyone can find a physical activity they enjoy and can practice throughout life. You could see my father jogging down the streets of Stillwater, Minnesota, well into his 70's.

As kids are taught and practice BSI techniques at home and in the classroom, make sure they make time daily to exercise their body as well. Teach them by your own example and help them find activities that they will enjoy for life. This can be Pilates, yoga, running, swimming, water skiing, biking, walking, meditation, or playing a sport with their friends. They should do it for their own personal well-being.

And I don't mean exercising hours per day. We simply want them to be active for 30 minutes a day at least four-five times per week. Why? Because without daily physical activity, their heart rate, blood pressure, and cholesterol could dangerously rise and cause pain, sickness, and disease. Maybe not when they are young, but they will physically pay the price later in life. It's hard to have a DreamLife unless they exercise both their mind and body. And there's a big bonus - taking care of themselves physically can lower stress.

Ah, stress. Stress can be both good and bad. "At times when a person gets overwhelmed, stress hormones such as cortisol and noradrenaline are released. They fire fast as they try to help the person adapt to what the brain perceives as a dangerous situation. Then the brain and the body return to normal," suggests Dr. Rajita Sinha, Director of Yale's Interdisciplinary Stress Center. This is good short-term stress.

Bad stress, on the other hand, can have a negative effect on the brain that can also be traced to weight gain or a weaker immune system. However, Dr. Horesh Bergquist says, "We can learn to control stress by learning intervention strategies and rewiring the brain and body." Some positive examples include reframing the situation, more sleep, laughter, close friendships, meditation and exercise.

Another harmful burden can be financial stress. In fact, the American Psychological Association says that stress over finances is often considered the number one cause of stress. "Almost half of Americans say they are increasingly stressed about their ability to provide for their family's basic needs." Per another poll, 7 in 10 respondents are very stressed about money, and only one in ten report that they are not stressed about finances. This is significant because financial stress is linked to health problems like depression and sleep problems."

You and your kids can reduce financial stress by creating budgets and getting out of debt. Most experts acknowledge that chronic stress from debt is not good for your health and that many people can benefit from outside assistance. These are suggestions Kid$Vest recommends as ways to turn your kid's financial life around as well. The fact that our methodologies also reduce stress is simply a bonus. Remember the resources in the apps section of the DreamLife PyraPuzzle like Mint.com, PersonalCapital.com or PowerWallet.com? They can help them budget and plan their way to reduced debt and stress. This will keep their bad stress levels under control.

Finally, in previous chapters we discussed what a serious problem student debt is for our youth. Many kids will be paying off student loans well into their forties and fifties. How can we expect them to become financially secure and have fun along the way, when debt payments negatively impact their lives for so long?

For example, CBS News Correspondent Dean Reynolds reports, "Diana Berkovits owes Columbia University a lot. She got a good education, made important professional contacts and ran up a student loan debt there and at Ithaca College that will keep her in hock for at least 20 years." Berkovits said, "What I realize now is that when I was eighteen I had no concept of what it would mean to go to a school that cost more, and what I would end up paying when I graduated." Her $80,000 in loans from her undergraduate and graduate school days are on the high end of the red ink. It's astounding, but student loan debt in this country is now greater than credit card debt.

Reynolds also shares a story about Cayce Rasmussen. She is a senior at the University of Illinois who's afraid to even calculate what she owes. "(I'm) Probably going to have to work a job that I don't necessarily want (to)," Rasmussen said. A well-known study conducted by Jesse Rothstein of the University of California, Berkeley, and Cecilia Elena Rouse of Princeton, confirmed that the amount of debt students take on determines their specific life paths. Their study concluded that those with high student loans often chose to work in corporations in the private sector to receive those high wages to pay back what they owed. Thus, they are not working at jobs they love, but ones they need to get out of debt. How much stress are these kids, now young adults, adding to their lives?

And that's not all. "It can affect a lot of choices, like when to buy a home or whether to buy a home, getting married, having kids, saving for retirement, and saving for their own kids' education," said Lauren Asher, President of the Institute for College Access and Success. For some perspective, "A $60,000 student loan at 6% over ten years will cost a graduate $666 a month at a total cost of $79,934. Stretch these payments out over an extended 25-year plan and the monthly payment is $387, but the total payoff rises to $115,975," says Mark Kantrowitz of Cappex (a website built to help kids pick colleges and find scholarships). I don't care how you slice it, that is a boatload of money per month for people probably earning an average of

$40-50,000 a year, if they are lucky. This is a negative long-term life-changer for most American kids who want a college degree!

We must also understand that students can't just walk away from school debt. Even if kids declare bankruptcy, Uncle Sam will not forgive these loans. He will find them and garnish their wages. The effect on your kid's credit rating could be devastating for years. And we already noted that a lower credit rating could cost them big time in higher interest payments on loans.

Would it surprise you to know that more than 40% of Americans who borrowed from the government's main student loan program aren't making payments? Since overall student debt in the United States just went over $1.2 trillion dollars, this is a huge amount of money potentially lost. While the government worries that many of these loans will never be repaid, we all know who will make up the slack—our kids will. Another financial crisis in the making!

Financial debt and stress can derail anyone's plan for financial independence. These problems can also turn a healthy mind and body into one with numerous health problems. Kate Ashford in her article for Bundle.com, suggests there are three potential ways to graduate debt-free. "A four-year degree doesn't have to mean two decades of hard-core debt." Here are Kate's three strategies for leaving school in the black.

- **Live at home, not on campus.** Yes, it's great to be on campus for the social benefits, but at what cost?

- **Finish your education sooner.** Take College Level Examination Program (CLEP) or AP exams in high school or summer classes in college to finish in three years.
- **Make smart choices.** If you can't make up your mind on what school to attend, factor in scholarships and/or in-state tuition to cut down on the costs. Remember, having school debt in your 40's or 50's is not a wealth embracing scenario.

Both stress and debt, which go hand in hand, can negatively impact our kids' lives. *The Kid$Vest Project* can help alleviate these financial wealth killers. First, by educating youth about the potential alternatives through our BSI techniques, and then, by alleviating future negative financial stress that could actually make them ill.

"Money can't buy happiness, but it certainly is a stress reliever."

Besa Kosova

SUMMARY CHAPTERS- WHAT WE ALL CAN DO!

Chapter

EIGHT

STEPS TO FINANCIAL FREEDOM

There is nothing more important than allowing all our youth to achieve successful and happy financial lives. Below are takeaways from the book that kids, parents, teachers, and others can follow, so that the American Dream is kept alive for future generations.

For Kids:

- "Know Thyself"– understanding your strengths (gifts) and weaknesses to better assess your best career path and passions.
- Understand your individual propensity toward "present bias" so you can trick yourself into

sometimes delaying instant gratification for a better long-term life.

- Set a plan for your career and income (*The Kid$Vest Financial Binder*) by becoming savvy about the DreamLife PyraPuzzle building blocks. Adjust your individual plan as you gain knowledge and experience.
- Set up a brokerage account and a Roth IRA as soon as you have work income and make it a goal to have $8,000-10,000, or as much as possible, in it before you graduate high school. Get help from your parents/grandparents if they have the means to help you. This will likely be the best investment you will ever make in yourself and your life.
- Become a Kid$Vest member to learn BSI skills and set up your Roth IRA, or do so with another financial organization. BUT DO IT NOW!
- If you are unsure about attending college right after high school, don't yet have career aspirations, or simply don't have the cash for college, think about taking a gap year after high school. You can work and gain experience to understand your passions and gifts, while funding your Roth IRA.

For Parents/Grandparents:

- Start teaching your kids about money and the power of compound interest at home via games, allowances, part-time jobs, and reading *The*

Kid$Vest Project. Offer one tidbit of financial health guidance each day to your child.

- Set up a 529 education fund the day your kids are born. The contribution dollar amount is unimportant at first. Remember that education is still one of the best routes to financial security!
- Begin gifting your kids/grandkids money during your lifetime, if you have the means. It's tax free up to $14,000 annually per spouse. Funds could pay college expenses, etc.
- Teach your kids the value of hard work and how part and full-time jobs in their teens can secure their financial success.
- Help your children set up Roth IRAs and brokerage accounts in their teens and either teach them how to fund them or help them do so up to $10,000 (or as much as possible) before they graduate high school. This will be the best investment you will ever make in your children's financial life (even more than a college education).
- Put pressure on your politicians and school boards to add financial literacy and human achievement skills (SEL) into our educational curriculums.

For School Administrators and Teachers:

- Make it a priority to add curriculum and specific classes that includes financial health—BSI information in your school district.

- Add personal finance programs into your classrooms, either directly or indirectly. Get help if you don't understand how to do so.
- In addition to financial education, learn the psychology behind delayed gratification, debt, stress, present bias, and exponential-growth bias (compounding) so you can begin integrating these important concepts into your class curriculums. You will become a better teacher if you do!

For Federal and State Governments:

- Make it a priority to add financial literacy programs throughout our educational curriculum for grades K-12 and beyond.
- Initiate programs like KidSave, where $1,000 is set up in an account at each child's birth and is used for education or retirement (proposed legislation by Senator Bob Kerry).
- Establish a Kid$Vest fund that allows kids to save from $8,000-10,000 in Roth IRAs, before they graduate high school. The fund should be a no or low-cost index fund that guarantees tax free interest of 5-6% until participants reach 65 years old.

For Wealthy and Philanthropic-minded Community Business Leaders and Individuals:

- Convince your local educational systems to include financial health training or use the Kid$Vest model in their curriculums.
- Make it a goal to offer financial advice to at least one child in your community daily.
- Offer part and full-time summer jobs or internships to kids.
- Assist kids in your community in setting up Roth IRAs and brokerage accounts in their teens. Then either teach them how to fund it, or help them fund it with $8,000-10,000, (or whatever they can afford), before they graduate high school. This will be the best financial investment you will ever make in your community's children.
- Work with local school boards, administrators, teachers, business leaders and students to bring *The Kid$Vest Project* to your community.

When you get where you're goin'
Don't forget to turn back around
Help the next one in line
Always stay humble and kind.

Tim McGraw, "Humble and Kind"

Chapter NINE

EPILOGUE

The Kid$Vest Model can absolutely be a financial game-changer for future generations of Americans. It will start slowly, of course, like a snowflake (Hey, I live in Minnesota). Then as more and more kids, parents, educators, and communities join, flakes will turn into a giant snowball. When momentum takes over it becomes unstoppable—and becomes an avalanche!

It all gets rolling as American Kids are taught by their parents and teachers to apply BSI techniques. I always say, "If you want to help America, start by helping Americans, all Americans." Kid$Vest could turn into an avalanche of financial security for millions of American kids who otherwise would not have an opportunity to obtain financial freedom.

Of course, this transformation won't happen overnight. Individual dollars invested will be small and almost unnoticeable at first, but as kids watch their portfolios grow it will ultimately change the way they view their lives and careers. Once portfolio growth takes hold, and the power of compound interest becomes apparent, the momentum picks up and entire communities may join in, making this financial avalanche grow larger and move faster. Finally, it becomes inevitable, particularly for middle and lower income families and their children.

There are barriers, of course, such as skepticism of the project's purpose, resistance to change by educators, unions and parents, lack of assistance from financial institutions, and community funding to support beta testing the program. And there will be kids who procrastinate because they believe there will always be time later to fulfill their financial goals.

Perhaps their situations are so dire that they have lost hope and they no longer believe they could ever become financially independent. My passion is to convince kids and their parents of the value and significance *The Kid$Vest Model* can have on their lives and our country's economic development.

What Might Dr. Martin Luther King Say?

Finally, with my deepest respect to Dr. Martin Luther King's famous speech on equality, I have a dream for all kids too. I dream that:

- All children are taught about BSI techniques at home and in our schools
- We make it a priority for all children to attend college if they desire, but at the proper cost and time in their lives
- Hard work and modest early savings and investments can positively change the way American kids grow up, work, play, and retire
- All American children will retire with class and dignity, no matter their career choice or trade

- In fifty years, the US middle class will continue to expand and the American Dream will still be alive and well

It has been an honor sharing my financial literacy ideas and The Kid$Vest Project with you. Thank you! I hope my lack of writing skill doesn't detract from the important issues and solutions I offer to resolve our significant American wealth-gap problem.

"Don't ever lose hope. Don't ever feel fear. You belong here, you got that? Keep working hard, because it's going to be so important now to be educated and focused."

Michelle Obama
Former First Lady
To a group of school kids

Addendum 1

THE KID$VEST FINANCIAL BINDER (KVFB)

The *Kid$Vest Financial Binder* (Strategic Financial Plan) includes all your kid's personal and financial information to keep track of their annual goals and financial success. Help them use this information to achieve their own individual DreamLife.

1. **Three Year Personal Assessment & Financial Goals Statement**
   A three-year rolling plan that keeps track of their goals and highlights their personal gifts and passions. This guarantees they will have a strategic plan and destination for their life.
2. **Service & Vendor Master List**
   Stay organized and efficient by listing all their personal vendors and financial accounts by name, contact information, and type.
3. **Net Worth Statement**
   Their personal net worth is tracked annually to review their overall financial success. Since Net Worth equals your assets minus your liabilities, the totals may be negative when kids are in their teens and twenties. No worries, because as they apply learned BSI skills and begin their career, this can turn positive quickly.
4. **Spending Plan (Budget)**
   Your kids create and track their personal spending plan. This allows them to monitor what they budget, save, and invest to make sure

their personal DreamLife comes true. Depending on their age or sophistication, they may later transfer this information to free electronic budgeting programs like Mint, Spending Tracker, or PowerWallet.

5. **Investment Strategy**
   As their investment expertise grows through time and experience, their investment style will emerge. This style will be based on their individual discipline, values, and risk tolerance. In their teens and early twenties, most of them will want to stick to simple, low cost index funds. They can customize their style as they become a more sophisticated investor.
6. **Credit Rating Information**
   A healthy credit rating allows your kids to borrow money as needed and at the best possible interest rate. Keeping track of their credit score via free credit services can save them thousands of dollars in interest over their lifetime.
7. **'Stairway to Financial Heaven' Calendar**
   We have identified steps parents and kids can take to ensure financial freedom. This checkup is the last section of their Financial Binder or Strategic Financial Plan to annually review and/or modify.

Note: Go to KidsVest.org to review The *Kid$Vest Financial Binder*.

Addendum 2
SPENDING PLAN EXAMPLE

Income	Amount
Take-home pay **(wages, tips or allowances)**	
Additional Income **(Side business, interest, etc.)**	
	Total Income

Expenses	Amount
Housing **(Rent or mortgage plus taxes and insurance)**	
Transportation **(Car payments, gas, insurance, tolls, etc.)**	
Utilities **(Heat, water, etc)**	
Subscriptions **(Cable, Internet)**	
Groceries	
Medical **(doctor, dental, etc.)**	

Expenses (continued)	Amount
Dining, travel, and entertainment	
Other discretionary spending **(Hobbies, personal care, etc.)**	
Debt payments **(Credit cards, student loans, etc.)**	
Savings, emergency fund, investments, and retirement **(Roth IRA)**	
Other	
	Total Expenses

Bottom Line (Income minus expenses)	Total

Addendum 3

KID$CLUB MEMBERSHIP ACTION STEPS

If you believe in *The Kid$Vest Project* and would like to help kids become a Kid$Club member or initiate a Kid$Vest program in your community, go to the Kid$Vest Website (Kid$Vest.org) and do the following:

- Have your kids take advantage of the financial education and videos the website offers.
- Have your kids become "free" Kid$Club Members so they receive weekly blogs, articles, and BSI ideas.
- Help them initiate a Roth IRA (and perhaps a brokerage account) to begin funding their saving, investment, and retirement programs.
- Have them share their financial stories of success and failure with other Kid$Club Members on our website - we can all learn together.
- Obtain a copy of the Kid$Vest Financial Binder to help your kids keep their financial plans "top of mind" and on track.
- Have them contact us to become a Kid$Vest advocate in their school or community. They can become part of the grass roots army that shares education and action steps to reduce the nation's wealth-gap.

www.KidsVest.org
Greg A. Fouks, HeadKid
GAFouks@KidsVest.org

CHAPTER TITLE: NOTES AND REFERENCES

Forward: America: The Greatest Country on Earth?

- Peter Coy, 'Debt for Life," Bloomberg BusinessWeek, 9/2012, page ix
- Google Consumer Surveys, GOBankingRates survey, date, page xi

Chapter 1: BluePrint to Financial Security

- Cameron Huddleston, chart of GoBankingRates.com regarding education and income, 2016, page 12

Chapter 2: The Need for Youth Financial Literacy

- Rex Nutting, article on American worker retirement savings, 4/2016, page 17
- Tamara Draut, Demos Research Group, article "*Generation Broke,*" 2004, page 17
- E. S. Browning, Wall Street Journal, article on Social Security, page 17
- Robin Thompson, *Budget-Wise Consulting, Inc.*, page 17
- Josh Mitchell, Wall Street Journal reporter on regarding *Student Debt* article, 4/2016, page 18

- Aimee Pichhi, CBS New article from Census Bureau tax data, 2/2017, page 20

Chapter 3: The Kid$Vest Model

- Liz Weston, NerdWallet, promoting Financial Health vs. Financial Literacy, Minneapolis Star Tribune, 4/2017, page 30
- Charles Schwab and Star Tribune articles, respectively, on entrepreneurial kids, page 52

Chapter 4: The DreamLife PyraPuzzle—Living A Life You Love!

- Alan Chapman, © 2007 Maslow Hierarchy of Needs' chart, www.businessballs.com , page 56
- Huffington Post article by Rebecca Klein, 5/2014, page 60
- MoneyWatch "How Many College Students Graduate." article by Lynn O'Shaughnessy, 2013, page 60
- Liz Weston of Morningstar, Graduate Earning Chart, Pew Research 2007, page 61
- Credit Rating charts, Home Buying Institute, page 84
- Robert Hauver, "Double D Widend Star Alert" Newsletter, page 91

Chapter 5: Life's Big Financial Moments

- USDA report on average cost of raising a child, 2013, page 115
- College Board report, 2015-2016, page 115

Chapter 6: So Just for Fun, How to Become a Millionaire

- "A Penny Doubled Every Day," example by Alan Yu, *page 121*
- Kimberly Palmer, U.S. News and World report, Michael Sherraden, University of Michigan Professor, 11/5/2009, page 128

A NOTE FROM THE AUTHOR

THANK YOU FOR READING *THE KID$VEST PROJECT*! I hope that it will help parents, teachers, and communities to inspire kids and students to become financially secure.

Please email your stories or comments regarding this book to GAFouks@KidsVest.org or mail them to:

Greg A. Fouks
24 White Pine Road, # 10
St. Paul, MN 55127

To contact me about possible speaking engagements or appearances, please visit me at www.kidsvest.org. or email me at GAFouks@KidsVest.org.

ABOUT GREG A. FOUKS

Greg grew up in Hudson, WI, and Stillwater, MN—two adjacent and beautiful river communities on the St. Croix River. As a senior, he won the Kolliner Award for the *most outstanding* student athlete and was inducted into the Stillwater Hall of Fame in 2007. He played college basketball for the Huskies at St. Cloud State University.

His career included leadership and management roles at Securian Financial, Marketing One, Tor Dahl & Associates and HRValue Group. He was an entrepreneur in the database management and executive search industries and hired over 2,000 employees, including over 150 C-suite leaders in the financial services industry.

His last position was as the President of the James J. Hill Center, the former reference library in downtown St. Paul, Minnesota. His team was responsible for transforming the Center into a business and entrepreneurial organization.

His 30 plus-years involvement in the financial services industry and his love of personal investing, has inspired him to write *The Kid$Vest Project*. He is hopeful that parents, teachers, and communities will invest time in educating all American kids how to budget, save, and invest in their dreams and become financially secure!